The

Nicola Baird is an environmental journalist based in London. She has written for *New Scientist*, *Financial Times*, *BBC Wildlife* and *Green Futures* and edits newsletters on forest management and genetics. Although she started driving at seventeen, she is now car-less by choice, preferring to get around by foot, bike or train. This is her fourth book.

Nicola Baird

The Estate We're In

Who's Driving Car Culture?

INDIGO

First published in Great Britain 1998
as an Indigo Paperback Original

Indigo is an imprint of the Cassell Group
Wellington House, 125 Strand, London WC2R 0BB

A catalogue record for this book is available from the British Library.

ISBN 0 575 40156 7

Lines from 'Autogeddon' reproduced with permission of Curtis Brown Ltd,
London, on behalf of Heathcote Williams. Copyright Heathcote Williams, 1991

'A13 Trunk Road To The Sea'. Words by Billy Bragg © 1984 Edwin H. Morris
& Co Inc/Burke & Van Heusen Inc, USA

Designed and typeset by Production Line, Minster Lovell, Oxford.
Printed and bound in Great Britain by
Guernsey Press Co Ltd, Guernsey, Channel Isles.

98 99   10 9 8 7 6 5 4 3 2 1

Over much of the world and in most of its cities the liberator, like many successful revolutionaries, is increasingly becoming an oppressor. Cars have reshaped landscapes and societies, killed millions through accidents and pollution, gobbled up scarce resources and marginalised the poor.

Geoffrey Lean, *Independent on Sunday*, 21 January 1996

Contents

Thanks to

Andrew Baird (computer mastery); Eliza Baird (organizing skills); Faith Brooker; Rachel Cooke, Kevin Davey; Julia Gallagher; Thomas Harding; Honey; Robbie Kelman; Andy Lees: Neil Macdonald; Reno Marioni; Pete May (ginger tea service); Mark McCallum; Samira Msaad; Peter Quaife; Hannah Scrase; Harley Sherlock; Adrian Thomas (guided tours); and Tom Wakeford. Also thanks for the use of the library at the Council for the Protection of Rural England, Islington Ecology Centre and Transport 2000.

CHAPTER ONE

Cars R us

This book does not blame car drivers for the state we're in. After all, anyone in a vehicle can be driven mad, every day, by the traffic. Cars are expensive to buy, insure and maintain; petrol is expensive; cars get broken into; parts are expensive; cars fail the MoT; no-claims bonuses are scrapped; other people's cars make you late; there's nowhere to park; other people inspire road rage; drivers can't drink; cars get written off . . . Buses clog up the roads. Buses don't even turn up. Taxis disappear when it's wet, sunny, late – or there's a big game on the box. Cycling isn't safe. The roads are dangerous . . . But the biggest problem of all is that there are just too many other people on those roads.

Traffic jams are so much a part of urban life that few road users expect to arrive in the time a journey ought to take. For most drivers it's a miracle when you find a car-parking space – and the right coins to pay for it. Author Emrys Jones puts this frustration well: 'No one has driven at snail's pace through London, already late for an appointment and with no guarantee of a parking place at journey's end, without cursing the road system; no one has approached Caracas or Rio through the awfulness of their shanty towns without wondering why they are tolerated; or seen the street-sleepers in Calcutta – or those under Charing Cross Bridge, for that matter – without being convinced that man has made his own hell.'[1]

The new improved hell came to our capital on 21 April 1997. London ground to a halt, with total city gridlock and queues on all the main routes into the capital. This mother of all rush-hour traffic jams, sparked by an IRA bomb scare, showed a society addicted to car ownership what twenty-first-century idling was going to be like. And it didn't like it.

But how can we expect to unclog roads now that three out of four people rely on their car for all journeys?[2] Although there are more than twenty-seven million cars registered in Britain, there could be forty million on the road by 2025.[3] Each August, when the registration letter changes, more than 450,000 new cars are snapped up.[4] In August 1997, when the UK was still releasing new numberplates annually, 526,000 new cars were bought. That's enough to bring a six-lane London–Edinburgh motorway to a standstill. By the time there are thirty-four million cars on the road, that imaginary motorway parking lot will be 140 lanes wide.[5]

More worryingly, cars – or rather the fossil fuels which power them – account for at least 22 per cent of the UK's carbon dioxide (CO_2) emissions. As CO_2 is one of the key greenhouse gases, traffic is clearly a major cause of global warming, the terrifying problem which threatens to change the world's climate irrevocably, bringing a nightmare of climate disasters for future generations.

Yet at the same time as the effects of traffic pollution are becoming better known, such as the increases in asthma and other respiratory problems, many companies are using ever more sophisticated marketing skills to shift cars and lobby for bigger roads. Brazil expects to see its home car market double to 2.7 million sales a year by 2004; the total growth for the

South American region could be five million.[6] Car sales in India
are growing at about 26 per cent each year – as a result Calcutta
looks set to build six new flyovers and ban non-polluting cycle
rickshaws to ease congestion in the city.[7]

The vested interests of the motor industry mean that time and
again pollution figures are deliberately fudged. For example,
Britain has repeatedly argued against tightening EU standards
on vehicle emissions and fuel quality. In exasperation a confi-
dential EU report finally did the dirty on the UK's clean, green
image. 'Far from making Britain the "clean man of Europe",
John Major's government has repeatedly argued against key
measures needed to further reduce the dangerous pollutants
being spewed into the air from car exhausts. The Danes,
Germans, Swedes, Austrians and Finns are the real clean men.
In dealing with traffic pollution, this report shows Britain still
languishing towards the bottom of the European league,'[8]
commented Friends of the Earth transport campaigner Roger
Higman, in response to a leaked report, in spring 1997.

Right to drive

We all want to drive, we all have a right to drive: and that's the
problem. Congestion during the morning and evening rush
hours – that growing time between 7 and 10 a.m. and 4 and
7 p.m. – already affects every urban centre. Rural traffic is set to
see yet more snarl-ups, often on roads with just a handful of
passing-places. Despite this, anyone with a set of car keys – at
seventeen, if you're lucky enough to pass your test first go and
have access to wheels – knows the world gets a lot more interesting in a car. For women it's freedom; for men a babe magnet –
a factor Jeremy Clarkson never fails to exploit in his testosterone-
charged reports for the massively popular TV shows *Top Gear*

and *Motor World*. You can flash a snazzy model; take off when you want (rather than wait for a lift); impress a hot date; buy heavy stuff at the supermarket; arrive late; leave early; drive to the golf course or the seaside; shift furniture; save on train fares; say goodbye to the bus; drive around Europe or hire a car anywhere in the world ... the possibilities seem limitless.

That's why, if you ask people what they'd do if they won the Lottery, most start their shopping list with a new motor – even highly paid footballers. West Ham midfielder Frankie Lampard Jr drives a BMW Compact, but if he won the Lottery he claims he'd 'Get my mum and sister new cars – then get myself one, too!' His colleague, full-back Tim Breacker, has a Renault and a similar mindset. 'The first thing I'd buy if I won the Lottery would be the biggest, fastest, largest, most powerful and expensive car on the market.'[9] Many footballers do just that anyway.

This human urge to make life easier and faster – and to flash cash – has resulted in an explosion of car use. The American taste for massive gas-guzzlers, measuring so many more square cubic metres than European and Pacific Rim models, must be due to that nation's unquestioning assumption that a big man has a big car. Which is why cars are so useful for social deceit, as Desmond Morris explains: 'The really serious status climber ... [needs] the genuine article, and must always go one step further than he can afford ... If he can afford a small motor car, he buys a medium-sized one; if he can afford a medium-sized one, he buys a large one; if he can afford a single large one, he buys a second car as a runabout; if large cars become too common, he buys a small, but wildly expensive foreign sports car; if large rear-lights become the fashion, he buys the latest model with even bigger ones "to let people behind know he is in front", as the advertisers so succinctly express it. The one thing he does not do is to buy a row of life-sized, cardboard models of Rolls-Royces and display them outside his garage.'[10]

Nowadays advertisers market cars as more than a status symbol, suggesting that the model for you is the one that will reflect your personality. As an eye-catching ad for one of Renault's new-generation cars, the Mégane Scenic, points out: 'Got a life? Get a car to put it in.' This car allegedly 'talks your language'. Talking to your car? Come on, no one does that, do they? Still, if you don't mind the silence you could always go for Honda's new CR-V, which considers itself the 'ultimate recreation vehicle', boasting a sixteen-valve fridge, shower and picnic table. With such a machine there's probably no need ever to get out of it, whichever beauty spot you drive to. The car has become a womb with a view. And we pamper it like a baby: buffing, waxing and polishing. We are the mother and valet – steaming the wheel arches, shampooing the door pads, adding trims, personalized numberplates and air fresheners. When it's scratched we get road rage. When it's criticized for causing asthma, pollution, noise and death, we defend it. Cars R us.

Election drive

Hence New Labour's 1997 election strategy deliberately targeting car owners. The impetus came from the man behind the Labour steering wheel, leader Tony Blair, after canvassing an electrician polishing his Ford Sierra during the 1992 election. 'Will you vote Labour?' asked Blair. The electrician claimed he couldn't: yes, he used to vote Labour, but planned to vote Tory now he was a home owner. For Blair this was a road-to-Damascus moment. He realized that, if Labour was going to get into government, then it was going to have to win back voters with a smart car parked in their own drive.

Dutifully the Walworth Road campaigners broke down the electorate into votes behind the wheel: writing-off Rolls-Royce men as Tory, Lada owners as Lib Dem and Citroën 2CV drivers as Greens. This left New Labour to concentrate on winning the confidence of everyone else, from Sierra and Mondeo owners to 'Galaxy Man' execs with their new multi-purpose vehicles.[11] Confused? Well, Stephen Bayley, using knowledge gleaned as motoring correspondent of the men's magazine *GQ*, shows why the choice of the £30,000 Galaxy shouldn't have been a surprise: 'If the Galaxy was a person it would be a fortyish graduate given to wearing deck shoes (probably with socks) at weekends, buying wine at Oddbins, chinos from Gap and possessing committed views on child-rearing, forests and third world debt. The Galaxy is New Labour on wheels.'[12]

'There's no conspiracy, people are not being conned – people *want* to get in cars,' explains Kerry Hamilton, Professor of Transport at the University of East London.[13] 'The people being asked to give up their cars don't want to inconvenience themselves by using public transport. It's made all the more hard because they often only get status from their car. They don't get status through their job, their home or their education. If you have money you buy respectability with a Rolls-Royce. Further down the line you get a second-hand BMW.'

Hamilton has been poking holes in our craze for private car use for years – she's done it for academics; she's done it with books, like her *Women and Transport*; and on Channel 4 with an exposé of Beeching's motives for axing the railways, in *Losing Track*, shown in 1984. 'In the 1970s people like me were seen as woolly hats, and more so the people in the fifties and sixties. Even now there are still people who say, "My life is impossible without a car." That's as irrational as saying, "My life is impossible without slavery",' says Hamilton, 'but certainly the road lobby is still convinced that the car is the saviour of the nation.'

That's why she feels that changing people's driving habits is 'not about getting the arguments right, we've done that. What's needed is a critical mass of people who operate together and lobby politicians for less cars. People making the most noise get the most attention.'

That's why time and again guides like *The Car, the Environment and the Economy*, produced by the Retail Motor Industry Federation, try to out-protest the protesters with calls for even-handed reporting of 'facts not fiction'. The federation argues that not only is the car essential to society but that the motor industry has made major efforts to fight pollution by reducing the amount of harmful emissions from car exhausts in recent years. 'The car has done more to improve the quality of life than any other invention in the past century. It provides the freedom, flexibility, convenience and comfort matched by no other form of transport . . . There is a direct linkage between GDP and the number of vehicle journeys. Greater economic activity, which creates more jobs and greater wealth, also creates the need for transport. Without a well-planned and maintained road system the nation's prosperity will be harmed.'[14] But as Mini-driver Mandy Rice-Davis might have pointed out, they would say that, wouldn't they?

A recent *Sun* editorial underlined this mood after Deputy Prime Minister John Prescott backed a report which suggested doubling fuel prices to drive cars off the road and reduce pollution. 'You can't force people to give up cars . . . People will use whatever form of transport suits them best. It's called freedom of choice.'[15] Until we start thinking differently, for most people freedom of choice equals a set of car keys. But it's a false argument: the average car costs at least £3000 a year to keep on the road;* they are a major noise nuisance day and night; they can only be driven by those with a licence (which means children are denied that 'freedom of choice', as are many older people); they make people sick; they aggravate asthma; they kill passers-by, passengers and other drivers; they pollute and choke our cities; they spoil the peacefulness of our countryside; and they keep on adding to the problem of global warming. Even so, we couldn't live without them. Could we?

First love

The car affair started well . . . The chairman of the Daimler Motor Company could boast on May Day 1896: 'We are celebrating the birthday of [one of] the most wonderful industries that God has ever blessed mankind with . . . since the world began . . . each large town will have its own factories, and Nottingham carriages will vie with Birmingham carriages for lightness, elegance and speed.'[16]

The car was not a British invention. There are tales that Leonardo da Vinci sketched a horseless carriage, and many people believe the original concept dates back to the Chan dynasty, more than three thousand years ago. So there's a certain irony that China has until recently been the country which swore by pedal power. In Germany Carl Benz and Gottlieb Daimler, each working independently but inspired by the bicycle and carriage trades, developed a car chassis. Yet it was a Parisian firm, Panhard and Levassor, which took up a

* RAC figures (July 1997) show that over a three-year period the annual cost of a new 1000cc car, using unleaded fuel, is £3479, or 29p a mile. A 2000cc car costs £6853 annually, or 57.1p a mile. Annual costs for diesel engines are higher: for 1000cc the yearly sum is £3805, or 31.7p a mile, and for over 2000cc it is £8435, 70.3p a mile.

licence to manufacture a V-twin engine, subsequently patented by Daimler in 1889. Car production had started. Around the same time groups that have become household names, like Peugeot and Renault, also got in on the act. As a result, by the start of the twentieth century France was the world's leading car maker. And Paris was the 'undisputed capital of the automobile world'.[17]

Coventry became Britain's first motoring city. Daimler was founded there in 1896 and produced Britain's first cars in 1897. The same year speed limits were changed, allowing cars to travel at 14 mph – previously it was 4 mph in the country, 2 mph in towns. The British motor industry grew from the success of the earlier cycle boom. Five major bicycle manufacturers, Humber, Sunbeam, Singer, Rover and Hillman, shifted their interest to cars. Britain was Europe's biggest motor-producing country in 1932, when she overtook France, staying in pole position until 1955. In 1950 Britain moved ahead of America to become the world's largest exporter of motor vehicles. In 1968, when British Leyland Motor Corporation was formed, it was fifth in world terms behind the American big three and Volkswagen. By 1987 the UK built 1.2 million cars but had slipped to fifth in the European production table, behind Germany, France, Italy and Spain. The next year it was ninth. The rise and crashing fall of Britain's motor industry has been well charted.

During those early years motorists had to fight for the right to drive. The venerable RAC was an early road campaigner although it began as an exclusive membership club in 1904. Meanwhile, the AA, according to author Mark Liniado, was 'formed in 1905, with the primary aim of subverting police traps'.[18] However, as time passed the AA developed a more citizen-friendly approach with the erection of road signs all round Britain, naming towns and villages as well as providing distances to the next village, a practice also adopted by the Cyclists' Touring Club. Their dedication paid off: nowadays driving is seen as normal behaviour and those challenging road-building or the right to drive as deviant.

There was even a national church-led celebration of the car's centenary, held at Coventry Cathedral because of the city's historic links with car-manufacturing. The start of the service backfired when smoke from the 1897 Coventry Daimler left the congregation coughing and choking as it was driven down the aisle. And to make matters worse the Provost, the Very Reverend John Petty revved up the service by asking God's forgiveness, in the first prayer, for the 'environmental pollution from exhaust fumes, the relentless encroachment of new roads into our countryside and the appalling toll of death and injury'.

Then a protest from a naked woman, daubed with anti-car slogans, put the brakes on car worship – as another naked lady, Lady Godiva, had protested a thousand years earlier. Angel, as the twenty-eight-year-old called herself, disrupted a display of the classic Jaguar E Type and Hillman Imp to shout out: 'The motor car is a killing machine! You are killing each other and you are killing the next generation. I am here to mourn the death of my mother and the seventeen million people killed directly by the motor car. And to remember the mothers who have lost their children, the orphaned children, our brothers, sisters, fathers and friends. Mother Earth forgive us.'

Perhaps the thousand car worshippers, who included the classic-car *aficionado* Prince Michael of Kent, felt Angel had a point on that bitter January day. The only light moment was when a gang of Coventry University students, banging together car parts as instruments, chorused: 'The car has another dimension I'm almost too modest to mention. It's a boudoir for lovers who smooch on the covers and sometimes destroy the suspension.'[19]

The challenge, now, is to find ways of getting our car-mad society out of its cars. Alternative and cheap transport methods, escalating petrol prices and guilt trips compete against the might of the road lobby, sophisticated car ads and the sheer convenience of your own wheels. Can we put a metaphorical bomb under car culture? Yes, some small changes by drivers could make roads less congested and street life better (and there are many ideas about this in these pages), but there are also strategic changes which need to be tackled, many at government level. That's why, from the anti-car lobby's point of view, it's poetic justice that Parliament Square, which faces the Houses of Parliament, is one of the most polluted spots in Britain.[20]

CHAPTER TWO

Car culture

From an aeroplane the patterns are the same world-wide: the straight roads, the snaking roads and the scenic roads, all flowing townward. In daylight you may see car parks, and houses with their neatly built garages, a sort of temple for the motor vehicle. Whatever the weather you will see roads – and they can be beautiful. At night, as you fly across international boundaries you can watch headlight stars flow along the illuminated monuments of twentieth-century archaeology – interchanges, arterials and spaghetti junctions. These are the roads heading to the desert city of Las Vegas; the chaotic roads merging in Mexico City; the jammed streets of Manila; the gridlock of downtown New York; and the choked ring roads of London. Once you've cleared customs and are parked in an airport cab it's easy to see you were fooled. Most roads go somewhere, but many more go nowhere fast.

At the motel you switch on the TV, and watch *Deals on Wheels* and a rerun of *The Sweeney* followed by the late-night movie, *The Italian Job*. Every programme is interrupted by ads offering womb-like security, or the chance to impress your ideal date in the latest runarounds. Even the news carries traffic reports. Outside your window, vehicles thunder past.

It's only the determinedly anti-car who can claim they're not affected by car culture: everyone else soaks it up every day. You don't even have to be a driver to be touched by cars. There are cult road movies; innumerable pop songs; collectors' magazines; Noddy models and Postman Pat everythings; drive-in McDonald's and drive-in cinemas; novels and stories about cars; urban myths; audiobooks; Grand Prix racing on the box; pictures; ornaments; and Dinky toys. Food guru Terence Conran has just named his new King's Road deli and café Bluebird, after the finned speed machine Malcolm Campbell drove to set the land-speed record of 174.883 mph on 4 February 1927.[1] But then he may just be recalling the building's past – it used to be a garage, as did the building which houses the Conran Shop, Michelin House.

Classic passion

Roger and Jill Hadlee know all about love–hate relationships with motors. Roger admits traffic is a scourge, but he loves to put his foot down. The couple moved house to escape the noise, and exasperation, of seeing a shared driveway designed for five cars from five households having to cram in sixteen vehicles – not counting visitors' cars. But since Roger hit fifty their new, joint passion has been vintage motors.

'We had a brand new Austin-Healey Sprite when we were first married. We were able to slip our eldest daughter's carrycot into the boot, but if she sat up she hit her head! So when more children came along we had to trade it in for a Mini van,' remembers Roger. After twenty-five years of family runarounds they decided to buy another classic car. One of their auction buys was an Aston Martin DBS from

Coy's auctioneers. 'I tried to hold his hand down,' remembers Jill, laughing, 'but he just put up the other.' After competing in the 1996 World Fiva Rally, they were hooked.

'The car is a toy,' admits Jill, 'but rallies are fun, and it's something we can do together – otherwise holidays are a problem as I'm a beach bum, whereas Roger wants an action holiday.'

They have just returned from a week in France with their much-loved 1953 Morgan. The Norman Conquest Rally – driving in the morning and sightseeing in the afternoon – suited them both well. 'It was a really good holiday; the serious rallies go on all day, but it's frustrating to go to really nice places and have no time to look around them. Also people are really friendly in France. The UK has a tremendous history of sports cars, so in a way they are quite common, but in France there are very few open cars,' adds Roger, who does all the driving. When I wonder why, Jill points out that: 'The clutch is like kicking a brick wall and as we tend to miss turnings there are a lot of clutch changes.'

Like many of the rally wives, Jill does the navigating. Things can go disastrously wrong amongst the rally maps – there are tales on the circuit of one wrong turn too many leading to an acrimonious divorce. And even though she enjoys the events, Jill admits that she 'takes more Nurofen on a rally than during the rest of the year. It's the stress of competition and,' here her voice drops to a whisper, 'the Morgan is very uncomfortable. If it rains the hood leaks like a sieve. That's when happiness is just a new plastic bag capable of catching the floods.'

A hundred years after the birth of the first British motor car a Classic Sports Car collection of stamps was launched. In the special presentation pack philatelists could indulge in admiration for the 20p Triumph TR3, the 26p MG TD, the 37p Austin-Healey 100, the 43p Jaguar XK120 and the 63p Morgan Plus Four.

'The car is unique: it's mobile, highly visible and a social currency everybody understands. We don't just admire cars, we're devoted to them: just look at the honeyed indulgence we show them when they're old,' explained the Royal Mail. 'Antique cars or classics are being polished and preserved like period pieces, as much a part of our social heritage as Coventry Cathedral and Formica worktops. You see, they're more than just the day before yesterday's technology. They're rolling reminders of the way we were. Take one look at the exuberance of these classic sports cars from the heyday of British motoring and you realise just how much the world has changed. There's an optimistic innocence and a belief in the future; the twinkling chrome promised so much. And it's precisely that happy vision of the future that now makes us misty-eyed.'[2]

In his book *Car Wars*, experienced PR guru John Butman tries to explain the myths: 'A car is more than a car: it reflects the priorities of the era, the country, the people that shape it. It also contributes to defining those priorities. It is both chicken and egg, leader and follower. More than any other consumer product, the car is three-dimensional shorthand for who and what you are. Thus the rise of national automotive stereotypes: the soft, superficial American; the spartan, ultra-engineered German; the bland, practical Japanese; the safe Swede; the stylish Italian; the idiosyncratic Brit. But these images are evolving too. From a product based on national obsessions, the car is beginning to reflect the changing requirements of a unifying world. The car must be more culturally neutral now, but also more narrowly focused by specific market segment – to appeal to the "sporting" set, for example, or to executive buyers or the affluent young.'[3]

You and your car

Your car will probably be the second most expensive purchase of your lifetime: only a house will be more – though it's perfectly possible to spend more on wheels than the place you live. That's why you don't have to be an anthropologist, or a car buff, to realize that knowing the car is knowing the person. Everyone understands that Mondeo drivers are middle-ranking salesmen; Renault 5s are driven by Sloaney students; Mercs by footballers; old Jags and Rolls-Royces by con men (well, they do cost around £120,000); BMWs by City types; whilst Royals, plus a plethora of movie stars including Tom Cruise and Jack Nicholson, opt for the classic four-wheel drives like Range Rover or the Land-Rover Discovery.[4] Jeremy Clarkson may be willing to have a hundred different makes of car in his driveway, but each gives a message: 'By computing the position of the stars on April 11, 1960, an astrologer would be able to deduce that I am selfish, arrogant and thoughtless. But this seems unnecessarily complicated. I mean, why bother with reference books and slide rules and telescopes when you can simply ask what sort of car I drive. See the car. Know the man.'[5]

The reason why some cars have such appeal – like the VW Beetle, the Citroën 2CV and the Morris Minor – is obvious claim authors Peter Marsh and Peter Collett: 'Psychologists and ethnologists have discovered that there are certain cues which trigger an innate caring response to young children and baby animals. Among such cues are a head which is large in proportion to the body, large eyes, rounded body shape, short thick extremities and rounded protruding cheeks. Cute cars seem to have many of these features. They are 'round' in shape . . . There is something about their stubbiness and the relatively large headlights which stand out underneath the curving forehead of the bonnet. Because they look like babies they evoke a special kind of bond. They are objects demanding loving care and devotion, and not surprisingly it is these kinds of cars which are most often given pet names and treated like one of the family.'[6]

In it together

'That's my baby,' says John Kane patting the dashboard of his VW Beetle proudly as we hit 75 mph. 'It's a great new engine,' he says, patting the dashboard again. The great new engine is also very loud and I have to get him to repeat everything he's said. To my embarrassment I discover he was talking to the car. When we go to overtake he makes clicking noises, as if he was encouraging a horse, though in the end he tucks back into his lane with a wry smile on his face. The old Beetle just isn't up to the headwind on the M5 – and there's still the crowded A30 to face. The surf ski strapped to the top doesn't help: we're going to take longer than ever to get to Cornwall. But John doesn't care. He does more than love his car, he really does thinks of it as a substitute kid. But at thirty-one years old, with its rather dented black wings and a beige body on to which John has carefully stuck, in neat black taped letters, the car's registration number, it's a strange beast to lavish parental affection on. But as the magazine for Beetle fans, Volksworld, *shows, there are plenty of car drivers mad for the Beetle.*

'People at work don't understand why I have a Beetle,'

*continues John, who nods reluctantly in response to the frantic
waves from any Beetle driver heading the other way. 'I take the
piss out of these Beetle owners that seem to think once you've
got a VW you turn into a warm, happy person,' he says,
shifting a little on the much-repaired leather driving seat, his
knees tight up to the steering wheel. 'I see my Beetle as the best
tool I can have. I don't want a modern car which will be worn
out in five or ten years. There's a Green angle too. Modern
cars are made up of a phenomenal amount of steel and rubber
and plastic. But the Beetle has no plastic, even when it's
finished,' and here he pats the steering wheel reassuringly,
'the steel can be reprocessed. Anyway, for me the Beetle isn't a
status thing, no one's going to drool over it like they would a
BMW or a Jag. It's tatty and it does look like a Noddy car, but
for people like me Beetles are brilliant. The mechanics are
simple so it's easy to work on, and if you can keep on top of the
rust you can keep a Beetle going indefinitely.' Though even he
admits there are faults: 'I can get fed up with trying to keep it
going. It doesn't like wet weather – at any rate the wipers are
too slow and the windscreen doesn't demist. It has terrible
lights, they are more like candles . . . Even so, it's worth
looking after.'*

Like John Kane, we all want our vehicle to be a bit more than
everyone else's boring modern car. We want it to be one of the
special ones. And to do that we can save up for a classic; we can
buy into a distinct clique – the Beetle, the 2CV, the MG with its
two-inch ground clearance; we can posh up with a black BMW;
or we can do what most people do, we can buy accessories.
Take that sun roof, soup up the power, customize its fittings,
order electric windows, stick on the go-fast stripes and add
messages, like the ubiquitous, MY OTHER CAR IS A PORSCHE or

the smug BABY ON BOARD. We don't want a car, we want a contender.

What you drive matters, especially on the day you want rid of it. At British Car Auctions and Central Motor Auctions the ubiquitous utility vehicles – often a fleet of ten to twenty white Vauxhall Astra estates – go under the hammer. And they go cheaply, not so much because of the miles on the clock, but because of their colour. 'It's a status thing,' says one regular auctiongoer. 'No one wants to look as if they are a photocopier engineer, except photocopier engineers, and even they would often rather have metallic.'

My grandmother, who reluctantly gave up her licence – in her eighties – after writing off her car on the A12, may call vehicles 'lethal litter', but she can't resist asking what visitors have parked in her Essex driveway. Drivers of top-of-the-range models receive a superior cup of tea. She understands that asking, 'Do you have a car?' is as irrelevant as saying, 'What do you do?' Better to save time and find it all out by asking: 'What do you drive?' These days it's a standard conversational gambit in many countries anyway, especially Australia.

On the road to nowhere

From the hitchhiker's bible, Jack Kerouac's *On the Road*, to Roddy Doyle's *The Van* or the wrong turning in Tom Wolfe's *Bonfire of the Vanities*, the road is used as much as a metaphor for progress, modernity and excitement as a device to keep throwing up new challenges, characters and situations. In America this pioneer culture started off on cine with the Western cowboys, but as horses lost the travel battle to wheels a very different genre of freedom-and-thrills appeared. The 'them against us' elements have stayed, though, in the road movie – it's fun in *The Blues Brothers*, but also think of the bloody ending for the bikers in *Easy Rider*, and for the characters in *Bonnie and Clyde*, *Thelma and Louise* and *Natural Born Killers*. Indeed, the latter allegedly sparked a series of copy-cat incidents in the US. Occasionally the cars get to star as the real baddies, as in *Christine* and *The Cars That Ate Paris*, providing a surreal parallel of the amount of death and destruction they precipitate on real roads.

The film that established the car chase as essential was a thriller starring Steve McQueen, *Bullitt*. McQueen plays a moody San Francisco cop assigned to protect a government witness. Fans of the film call it fast-moving, but the action could just as easily be called downright confusing: all seems to be leading to the moment when the safety belts are fastened with a click. What follows is the ultimate tyre-squealing, 100 mph chase around the hilly streets of San Francisco before the film climaxes in an inferno as the rammed baddies' car explodes at a gas station. That's not the end, but the best bit is definitely over.

Bullitt, which was first shown in 1968, turned McQueen into a superstar – despite one of cinema's most celebrated boobs, as obvious as the lights and camera stands that pop up throughout episodes of *Dr Who*. Look closely during the famous car chase and you can see McQueen's Mustang going past the same green VW Beetle again and again.[7]

The film was directed by a Brit, Peter Yates, who is proud of his much-imitated car chase, realizing that 'a great sort of mystique has grown round it'.

In another life McQueen might well have chosen to be a motor-bike racer or a Formula 1 driver, claims Barry Norman in his book *The Film Greats*. As it was, he was a member of the American team in an international six-day motor-bike trial in

Germany in 1964. Whilst off the set during the shooting of *The Great Escape*, in Germany, he famously stepped out of a wrecked Mercedes saying, 'Tell them to send me a red one next time.' Another night he spent driving from the set to the Italian border and back – at speeds of 100 mph all the way. According to John Sturges, who directed *The Great Escape* and was intended to direct another chase film where McQueen showed off his driving skills, *Le Mans*, McQueen did not have a death wish. 'Anybody attempting to put forward a creative effort is under a strain. There's a sense of frustration. Well, some people get rid of that by doing exercises, some by playing tennis, some by getting drunk. Steve drove a car.'[8]

Star of the controversial movie *Crash* (originally a book about getting sexual thrills from, er, coming off the road), James Spader is a typical car obsessive. 'I could talk about cars all day,' he says. He drives Porsches, sleek modified Porsches. He has an aluminium briefcase where he stores his driving music. There are songs to drive north and songs to drive south. He only does movies to finance his love of driving. He drives for days, from New York to New Orleans, from LA to New York, up to Utah, down to Florida, around Colorado, Highway 101, Route 66. Drives in, drives out. 'He doesn't criss-cross America in order to draw conclusions . . . He doesn't make any demands, he just likes the driving . . . "I love the idea that you are always in your vehicle. You are living in your car. It's great."'[9]

Part of the appeal of cars is that they let you travel through time. Driving puts you into your own road movie. Little wonder that all kids are introduced young to car drama. The ad men even play along to it, showing a small boy boasting, 'My dad's car is better than your dad's car.' But most start even younger, on their parents' knees, with *Chitty Chitty Bang Bang*. But they soon move on. By the time they're in long trousers their affections will have switched to the Batmobile. In *A Perfect World* the allure is spelt out when Kevin Costner tells the little kid that the car they are in is a time machine: 'Behind us, that's the past. Out ahead – that's the future.' We may have stopped believing in tooth fairies and Santa Claus, but it's hard to kill the notion that a trip in a car has the potential to lead to a much more significant journey... After all, on screen it always does: think of *Paper Moon*, *Rain Man*, *Priscilla, Queen of the Desert*, *Soft Top Hard Shoulder* and the study of three brothers finding out if they drive or are driven in *Coupe de Ville*.

Some of Disney's top-grossing family films feature a remarkably clever VW Beetle. It's in *The Love Bug* that Herbie is introduced as a little car with a mind of 'his' own. He picks his new owner – a racing driver down on his luck; repeatedly spills oil on his raceway enemy's foot; whimpers like a dolphin; and, in a very human gesture, nearly throws himself into San Francisco Bay when his driving partner tries to dump him. Herbie is also very, very fast. So speedy in fact that after his *Love Bug* victory he ends up in at least three more films, including a starring appearance at Monte Carlo.

What's fun about *The Love Bug* is that Herbie's driver refuses to admit Herbie's part in the success. Of course the viewer knows Herbie's role, even though in real life it shouldn't be possible. So when the driver, Jim Douglas, ponders about the relationship between cars and men the film's working well on two levels. 'There's been a lot of gloop written about the bond between a man and his automobile,' says Douglas. 'He showers gifts on it in way of accessories, gets hysterical if someone scratches the paint or makes it lose face on the freeway. Maybe some of these feelings get in the machinery?' echoing a wiser character, played by Buddy Hackett, whose time in Tibet had made him cotton on to Herbie's money-spinning, race-winning, endearing ways: 'We make machines and stuff them with information until they're smarter than we are. Take a car, most guys spend more time and money on a car than they do on their wife and kids in a year. Pretty soon the machine starts to think it is a somebody . . .'

Horror movies

Society's refusal to acknowledge the carnage that occurs daily on our roads is parodied in the surreal horror film *The Cars That Ate Paris*. This cult Australian movie, directed by Peter Weir (famous for the very spooky *Picnic at Hanging Rock*), focuses on the antics of the outback town of Paris. With a little help, visitors unfailingly crash on the outskirts of Paris. Car-body parts get recycled amongst the residents whilst crash victims are shunted along to the hospital for experimentation. 'It's not very pleasant, but that's the world we live in. That's the world of the motor car!' says the Mayor brusquely, his moustache twitching. The final bloodletting – hours before the car gymkhana – takes the horror offstage and into our own world, with its clear message that those who live by the car shall surely die by the car.

Heavy traffic at the music store

The car has been as omnipresent in rock music as it has on the screen. It turns up in everything, from the jaunty pop of Madness's 'Driving in My Car' ('It's not quite a Jaguar . . . Beep. Beep') to every heavy metal band intent on writing a tribute to their macho dream machine. Take the lyrics to Deep Purple's 1970s song 'Highway Star' – 'Nobody gonna steal my car . . . Ooh, it's a killer machine, it's got everything . . . I'm a highway star.' What bloke needs to stuff a sock down his tight

Street Fashion

The dramatic transformation of Methley Terrace – from a car-choked rat run to a green public garden – made all the nationals. But road makeovers are more common than journalists would lead us to believe, and they are mostly engineered by the film industry.

Much of the movie *Fever Pitch* was shot in the roads ring-fencing Arsenal FC's Highbury ground. For two weeks during the filming, a Union Jack was draped over the nursery sign, and parking spaces abounded – though they were off-limits for anyone not driving seventies motors, such as Morris Minor vans. London Docklands has even been used for the Vietnam War scenes in *Full Metal Jacket*.

Another London site that regularly gets the makeover treatment is Worship Street in EC1. Dingy and hemmed in during the day by tall, drab, flat-fronted blocks, it can be transformed into downtown New York in a couple of hours once the office workers leave for home. Up go the one-way signs; out come the *New York Post* vending boxes, mailboxes and fire hydrants turning pavement into sidewalk; down goes the carpet to remove all traces of British double yellow lines. As a finishing touch the street is then parked up with real American gas-guzzlers and patrolled by the obligatory yellow cab. It's such a perfect transformation that when you watch, say, Tom Cruise and Nicole Kidman's film *Eyes Wide Shut* it's impossible to believe just where some of the scenes were shot. The only clue that it's not the real Big Apple is the absence of discarded paper cups – this fall's designer litter.

leather trousers when he could pitch up at the car lot and buy a penis extension for the road?

It's often been joked that Bruce Springsteen has never written a song without parking a car in the lyrics. The cover of his seminal *Nebraska* album shows a view from a car windscreen of a vast sweep of flat empty country either side of a clear road. The road is bleak, but there's also a kind of freedom and poetry to be celebrated just by the act of driving through it – or so Bruce would have us believe. That's why Springsteen's car-centred songs capture blue-collar Americans' ambitions so perfectly. In 'Used Cars' he says it all: 'Now mister, the day the lottery I win I ain't never gonna ride in no used car again.' The new car is where it's at. He even shows how life's dramas are acted out on the highway. 'Highway Patrolman' tells the story of a divided family as a police sergeant chases his criminal brother, who's left a man in a pool of blood at a service station, across the state border.

But it is 'Open All Day Night' which signifies how important cars are as the ultimate American pulling machine. It's not so much a set of song lyrics as a DIY mechanics manual, with its description of having the carburettor cleaned and checked, propping the car up in the backyard on concrete blocks for a new clutch plate and a set of chocks, then a trip down to the carwash to check the plugs and points. Finally, the vehicle 'hummin' like a turbojet', Bruce informs us, 'I'm goin' out tonight, I'm gonna rock that joint'.

Even a sensitive singer/songwriter like Paul Simon is seduced by the pull of the car. In his 1983 song 'Cars Are Cars' he remembers how he once had a car that was more like a home, lived in it, loved in it and polished the chrome. Evidently, if some of his homes had been more like his car, he 'probably wouldn't have travelled this far'.

Virtual control

But why just *listen* to the message? You can turn Great Britain into Little England using a computer. Mark's CD-ROM, *Microsoft AutoRoute Express*, came free with his Pentium PC – and already he's wasted hours criss-crossing counties on it. Outside, his sporty red Corrado 16v is immobile, off the road because the security alarm has drained the battery. Inside, behind the wooden shutters, he faces the computer screen scanning travel articles, planning mini-breaks, printing out personalized itineraries and ticking off prime tourist sites. We go from Bournemouth to Whitley Bay, from the start of the A1 to Northallerton in Yorkshire, via a stop-off at Lincoln. The 143-mile journey from London to Lincoln should take two hours and thirty-eight minutes, clocking up an ETA of 17.02. 'That's a good time,' muses Mark as he zooms in for a 360° guided tour around Lincoln Cathedral, 'just in time for tea.' We imagine Earl Grey, scones and cream, the ticking of a grand-father clock, and just outside the ivy-girt bay window a parked red car, waiting to go.

Armchair travelling is addictive, as any fan of *National Geographic* magazine knows. Fantasy car travel is even better: the roads are clear and it's forever fog-free – the CD-ROM shows an inviting ribbon of open road winding across a green valley framed by gentle hills. We check out the motorway service stations *en route*, look up accommodation and scan travel articles. The only things the map doesn't show are railway stations – or the other people on the roads. It's a blind spot repeated over and over by the motor industry and ad men.

Poetry of motion

Car adoration is a spectacular – and expensive – love affair between man and machine. This passion is expertly captured by Kenneth Grahame in the children's classic *Wind in the Willows*, when Toad sees his first automobile. "'Glorious, stirring sight!" murmured Toad, never offering to move. "The poetry of motion! The real way to travel! The only way to travel! Here today – in next week tomorrow! Villages skipped, towns and cities jumped – always somebody else's horizon! O bliss! O poop-poop! O my! O my!'"[10]

Such passion keeps the specialist bookshops well stocked, like Motor Books near London's Leicester Square, and Chater's of Isleworth, which have been selling to the motoring

---

Net attack

Society's car malaise was denounced – appropriately – at the bizarrely old-fashioned Horse Hospital Club, just a few streets away from London's British Museum, a week before the Motor Show, 1997. The early clubbers could see that car culture was a wreck as they sipped mineral water and Freedom beer. Scary posters: WHAT GOOD IS SPEED IF THE BRAIN HAS OOZED OUT ON THE WAY – KARL KURTZ and DRIVING WITH YOUR LOVED ONE IS LIKE BECOMING ONE BODY . . . THERE IS NO ESCAPE FOR THE OTHER, NO ACTION TO BE TAKEN, WE ARE ONE, WE ARE WILLING TO DIE TOGETHER decorated the walls. In the corner *Bullitt* flickered across the TV, to its left was a massive projection of a crumpled yellow Cortina. All that was missing was the smell of gasoline.

And there, off the cobbled street and up on the first floor reached by a ramp designed to stop horses slipping, the east London art gallery, Camerawork, was launching its newly commissioned Auto-da-fé websites. *Requiem for the Car* (http://www.channel.org.uk/metropolis) and *roads&cars* (http://www.camerawork.net/roads&cars) are superb. *Requiem*, created by Akke Wagenaar, acknowledges: 'I really hate cars – except when I am inside one.' It tells the story of how even when she gave her car away to friends in Senegal, so it would have a collective use, she couldn't rid herself of the love–hate relationship.

Scrolling through *roads&cars* the computer pages move from left to right (not up and down) as if you are driving, whilst the menu bar has been converted into a dashboard by adding what looks like a milometer. In fact it's counting the number of finished cars rolling off the production line. Devised by Adrian Harris and Garry Samett, this website can provide a quiet drive around the anti-roads protest movement, hook into car manufacturers' websites or allow you to horrify yourself with statistics. Best of all, you can safely drink and drive.

As the DJ revved up on driving sounds with Grace Jones's 'Pull Up to the Bumper, Baby', I glanced at the car counter on the new *roads&cars* website: 8253 new cars had rolled off the assembly line over the past nine hours. By the time we'd driven the few miles home, another forty were waiting for buyers.

Camerawork is at 121 Roman Road, London E2 (0181 980 6256).

enthusiast for forty years. Some of the auto magazines, like *Cars and Car Conversions* (better known as *CCC*), also run book clubs. Can a bookshelf be complete without *CCC*'s recent book of the month, *Sporting Peugeot 205s: A Collector's Guide*?

Of course cars ram their way into many novels, but one of the most powerful images of cars fuelling our isolation is created by the notorious author Will Self in his short story 'Scale'. The protagonist, based in a Buckinghamshire dormitory town, is writing a thesis on the M40. And it seems to be this, as much as his morphine habit, which is doing his head in. Every now and then he takes an overview of England – as if he was in a car offering an aerial perspective – and sees that what were once carriageways on the road network are, twenty thousand years on, ley lines marching towards spiritually significant junctions. Where once was a service station there's now a burial site: 'The motorway tribe was divided up into clans or extended families, each of which had made its encampment at a particular junction and taken a different item of the prehistoric road furniture for its totem. My clan – Junction 2, that is – had somehow managed to preserve a set of cat's eyes from the oblivion of time.'[11] Self is setting up a scenario which has a chilling resonance for the commuter clan who make the same journey up and down the motorway Monday to Friday, isolated from anything but their own private miseries. OK, they can listen to the radio, play their own tapes or just enjoy their own company – but motorway driving can also be dull, dull, dull.

The poet Heathcote Williams hates the influence cars have over our world. He questions who's steering who in our car-loving culture by claiming:

Were an Alien Visitor
To hover a few hundred yards above the planet
It could be forgiven for thinking
That cars were the dominant life-form,
And that human beings were a kind of ambulatory fuel cell,
Injected when the car wished to move off,
And ejected when they were spent.[12]

He's wrong, of course.

Ben Elton's vision in his best-selling novel, *Gridlock,* is less bleak. 'All week people sit in traffic jams. Sometimes, on a Friday night, they go to the movies, on the way they sit in more traffic jams, they miss the first part of the movie because they can't find a parking place. Then they sit in a dark cinema and watch a man drive a car through rush-hour traffic, clear across a city at 80 miles an hour. If the man had turned into a six-foot banana we would say it was a stupid movie, but a man driving a car through a crowded city at 80 miles an hour we not only accept but remark to each other how brilliantly done the car chases were . . . The fact that if you actually tried any of that stuff for real you would not get 20 yards before ploughing into a bus queue and killing 30 innocent pedestrians, is not a part of the equation . . . Movie car chases remind us of how much we love cars. When the movie is over, everybody goes and sits in a jam again.'[13]

Box junction

This misplaced admiration is wittily summed up by the motoring industry proverb, 'Nobody waxes their fridge on Sunday morning.' Even off duty, we want to be with our cars. That's why the TV garages a range of car programmes, from live Formula 1 racing through to weekly shows like *Top Gear,* *Motor World* and *Deals on Wheels*. Other car shows have had success too, such as Channel 4's *Ride On*. And there are magazines aplenty, with titles like *The Automobile*, *AutoSport*, *Vintage Roadscene*, *What Car?*, *Model Auto Review* and the racy *Max Power* – a sort of auto *Loaded* which bills itself as 'the definitive guide to arsing around in cars'.

Where better to arse around in cars than Essex, which became known in the Thatcher years as the car county extraordinaire? Essex man drove an XR3 (too fast) on his London commute. The less affluent had to make do with a Ford Cortina, but they still voted Tory, lived in Basildon, did something in the City and vied with friends to get their hands on the first mobile phone. What Essex man wanted was loadsamoney, a mock-Tudor mansion – a few miles from the motorway – and a Page 3 stunner. Essex girls got so used to looking for love in a motor that a cache of car jokes spread, such as: 'How does an Essex girl turn the light out after sex? She shuts the car door.' Ford, clearly alert to Essex wit, has called its new model 'Ka'. 'Mota' could have been a close runner-up.

Although Essex isn't all bad, it's a place where conspicuous consumption is a mark of progress and where roads are still revered. This is the county where you are your car. That's why it has such dreadful public transport, other than the rush-hour commuter trains into London. To my mind the absolute worst of these roads is the A13. Yet it's a road which inspires strange passions amongst the Essex set – and has even built up a fan club, as if it was as scenic or as long or as special as America's first coast-to-coast highway, Route 66.

Essex man's road, the A13

So where does the A13 go? As Billy Bragg so memorably sang:

When you ever have to go to Shoeburyness
Take the A road, the OK road, that's the best
Go motoring on the A13 ...
Take in Fords, Dartford Tunnel and the river too
Go motoring on the A13.
It starts down in Wapping.
Then without stopping bypass Barking and straight through
　　　Dagenham
To Grays Thurrock and rather near Basildon
Pitsea, Thundersley, Hadleigh, Leigh on Sea
Chalkwell, Prittlewell and Southend on Sea ...
And if you ever go to Shoeburyness
Take the A road, the OK road, that's the best.

Bragg is parodying the well-known paean to Route 66 – a road which has its own fan club and a regular magazine. But even he can't hide the fact that the A13 is nothing more than a grim dollop of tarmac slicing through car country past shabby pylons, oil refineries and garages.

After Wapping, home of the ultimate phallic building, the flashing Canary Wharf, the A13 heads past Ford's and through hideous Dagenham. It crosses the M25, the motorway that was wrongly billed as the end to the commuter crush (and which may be widened even further). At Junctions 30 and 31, just north of the Dartford Tunnel, there's the ultimate Essex pit stop, the south-east's largest shopping centre, Lakeside, deliberately built as a drive-in temple of consumerism. Gleaming white, Lakeside looks as if the architects thought they'd been asked to do an Inca palace.

On a Saturday, Lakeside is packed with serious shoppers willing to blow their salaries on filling their fake-leather shopping bags. From the distance this vast complex seems to nestle into a large hole – presumably a gravel pit used to help build the nearby M25 and Essex arterials. At its deepest point there is still a lake, which is now surrounded by a shopping pavilion. Although there are other ways to get there, the obvious approach is by car. There are, after all, twelve thousand free parking spaces located around Lakeside. They could cope with just about all the vehicles owned by every member of the Environmental Transport Association.

Inside there are fountains near the door to the toilets; shopping lockers for those whose spending reduces them to a bag lady; and a floor plan to help take the nouveau Lakeside visitor from the House of Fraser to Bentalls, via Gap, River Island and Jeffrey Rogers. People obviously like it so much that they've thrown coins into the water, as if this was the Trevi Fountain in Rome that they long to visit again.

To remind Ms Essex that Tilbury Docks are near, at Lakeside the vowel O Europeanizes the cafés. Milky mugs of coffee become cappuccino and café latté at the Café Giardino, and there's even a snack bar called Jeff de Bruges. When they tire of Essex sophistication the girls get back to serious shopping, slipping in and out of leopardskin tops as deftly as they defy the laws of balance in their white high heels as they step in and out of the Essex motor, the Ford Escort.

At the central dais teenagers in identical Sporty Spice tracksuits, big shoes and dyed hair queue Saturday away for the chance of a makeover and snap at *Sugar* magazine's Face of 1998 contest. Next week Henry Cooper will be doing his stuff, and not long afterwards the carol singers will be shaking their tins as Lakeside moves up a gear for the Christmas shopping extravaganza.

The car culture even gets into the shopping mall. There are auto shops, of course: a Vauxhall Corsa Breeze is being raffled from Tony Le Voi Motors and brightly coloured plastic toy cars, big enough for a toddler to sit in and steer, are being rented out at £2.50 an hour.

When a child walks past clutching a balloon with the words VIRTUAL REALITY stamped on it, I know it's time to hit the road again. Just before the turning for the new town of Basildon and just past the Auto Raceway at Thurrock, the Highways Agency has set up a large blue sign: £160M NEW ROAD NETWORK, boasting of its mission statement, 'Investing in roads.' Here roads are something to boast about.

God knows why, the gateway for Basildon is really a new Beefeater, facing a crumbling weatherboard church. Its grandest buildings are country clubs. Go posh round here and you end up at Watt Tyler Country Club or Pitsea Country Club – pubs for members who drive to play a round of golf.

Suppose you lived near the A13, say in Harlow, or *on* the A13, in Basildon, what would you do besides cruise around Lakeside? Well there's the Indian takeaways, the trips to the garden centres, the sports centre, the fireplace shops and the pier. You'd go to the showrooms when you wanted to upgrade your motor; the MOT centre annually and the garage once a week. You'd buy stone eagles and cement them on to your gateposts; you'd listen to the traffic updates on Radio Essex (95.3 FM). You'd get stuck in jams, go to the mobile-phone centre, buy skateboards for the kids and park at the multi-storey. You'd shop at Argos or any of the big superstores along the road and you'd dream of trading in your runaround for a decent 4x4 at any of the garages which line the road. Here four wheels good, two legs bad.

It's a bleak industrial landscape – flat and crowded – and it stays that way until the A13 slips out of dual carriageway and throws drivers into the traffic queues signalling that the car parks of Southend are full.

Suddenly the electric pylons disappear and in their place are traffic islands, traffic lights and lines and lines of car showrooms, workshops and petrol stations. There are thousands: Compact Services, Fletchers, The Pitstop Café, a Ford showroom, the American Car Company, Auto Car Exchange, Elite Motors, Murray Motors, Godfrey Davis Garage, London Car Telephone, a BP garage, GMC Garages, National Garages, Kwik Fit, Car Choice, London Road Motors and the ultimate Essex showroom, Lookers – you can almost see *EastEnders'* Frank Butcher, David Wicks and Roy Evans on the forecourt. Buy now, pay later! Surely, even in Essex, no one could buy this many new motors? It's all very Arthur Daley. The A13 reveals a way of life, and that life is Little Detroit, Essex.

Finally the road ends, ingloriously at a roundabout near the shabby beach huts of Shoeburyness. In the distance is Southend's mile-long pier, and about as far away is the sea. Half the beach is sticky with estuary mud. Yes, Billy Bragg did a fine job immortalizing the A13. Surely even Bruce Springsteen, the rock star with the soul of a petrol-pump attendant, couldn't have done better.

CHAPTER THREE

Dead time

Because we all have a right to drive whenever we want, wherever there's a road, getting around is paradoxically becoming less easy. By far the most painful travel tales come from commuters: those brave humans who defy logic by travelling at exactly the same time to exactly the same place twice a day.

The specialists in forecasting trends, the consumer consultants at the Henley Centre, dub the time we spend getting to the office, the gym or the shops 'dead time'. 'Full time workers spend an average of nearly five hours commuting to and from work each week. Approximately 80 per cent of all commuting in the UK is car-related and 70 per cent of all leisure-connected travel involves a car. Of all the passenger kilometres travelled in Britain in a given day, almost 90 per cent involved a car . . . For many, distance is conquered by enforced patience rather than speed. Congestion and delay are endemic to the lives of millions of commuters. The really striking feature is just how much of this we are willing to withstand – the faddishness of road rage apart – before we abandon our cars.'[1]

Brits, famed for their orderly approach to standing in line, now sit and queue in the jams. Some actually enjoy it: they have time to themselves, with no boss or family making demands, and pass the time by listening to the radio, learning a new language or using the mobile phone. Today's cars have it all: drinks holders, cigarette lighters and electric seats to keep your bum warm. They only need a toilet to become a real home from home. In some places these are essential – no drive through Bangkok is complete without a portable 'comfort' potty. But a close look at the side of the motorway will reveal what motorway workers know to be the current solution to being caught short: you just wee into a plastic bottle and then lob it out of the window. Remember, if you come across one of these bottles, that it is not apple juice. On some stretches of motorway hard shoulder, bottles outnumber the strips of black tyre treads – you can get the kids to count them in a modern version of pub cricket.*

And even if there is a growing trend for working at home, which cuts down on commuter traffic, pollution and essential pit stops, it's still in its infancy. Currently only 4 per cent of people are full-time teleworkers – though the Henley Centre expects this to increase to thirteen million by 2010.[2]

However, for most commuters their journey is dictated by Hobson's choice – if they don't take what's offered, however bad, then there's nothing at all. Few long-suffering commuters would be surprised to learn that the phrase 'Hobson's choice' was coined by travellers using Thomas Hobson's infamous stables back at the turn of the seventeenth century. In modern times Hobson would have had a choice of career: second-hand car salesman or officious minicab boss. Back then customers at

---

*In pub cricket you divide the occupants of the car into teams. Points are collected by spotting a pub first and then receiving one point for each leg on the pub's signboard. For example, the Black Bull earns four points (for four legs).

his livery yard had to take the sad nag offered, or do their journey on foot. It was a deal which worked well for Hobson, who survived into his late eighties.

Britons have a bad habit of driving everywhere. After all, few people need to buy a car to get their daily paper or a pint of milk, but as more than half of all car trips are under five miles it might seem that most of us assume that we do. As a result we all suffer jams and gridlock on the roads into our major cities and towns. The CBI claims this congestion costs businesses and the economy about £19 billion a year – that's around £800 a household.

Streets made for driving

French intellectual André Gorz pointed out more than twenty years ago: 'The truth is, no one really has any choice. You aren't free to have a car or not because the suburban world is designed to be a function of the car – and, more and more, so is the city world. That is why to do away with the car in favour of the bicycle, the streetcar, the bus and the driverless taxi is not even applicable any longer in the big commuter cities like Los Angeles, Detroit, Houston or even Brussels, which are built by and for the automobile. These splintered cities are strung out along empty streets lined with identical developments; and their urban landscape (a desert) says, "These streets are made for driving as quickly as possible from work to home and vice versa. You go through here, you don't live here. At the end of the workday everyone ought to stay at home, and anyone found on the street after nightfall should be considered suspect of plotting evil."'[3]

'It is not only the financial costs of congestion, but also the frustration of time wasted and opportunities foregone, as you sit trapped by tailback after tailback, day after day, that makes this mounting congestion all the more intolerable,' claimed Andrew Smith MP, when he was a Labour transport spokesman.[4]

Three journeys to work:
'It's my life – but it's not ideal'

Clapham to White City, London

Gill Smith is a journalist who lives in Clapham, south London, and works at White City. On the map the distance is a few miles, but in her company car, a Citroën Saxo, it sometimes takes two and a half hours. 'Sometimes it would be quicker to walk. During term time, it's a nightmare,' she says.

'My house is five minutes' drive from a bridge, but it can take forty minutes to get there. I'm quite a volatile person and I do find driving stressful, and though the car's got a catalytic converter and runs on unleaded petrol I worry because I read that you get more fumes just sitting in a car than walking past. Anyway I'm contributing to the horrid noxious mêlée up in the sky. One of my nephews has got bad asthma, and that's aggravated by traffic pollution. I'm not one of these people who've got a car and who think, 'I don't care.' I do feel guilty and mean driving on my own. Sometimes I pick up a colleague, and I wonder if I should pick up people waiting at bus stops, but what if I pick up a mad axe murderer? Perhaps it would be different if I was a bloke, but then they might think I was a pervert!'

Despite these concerns Smith has no plans to go underground again: 'I've spent eighteen years taking public transport to work. The past three and a half on the Northern, Victoria and Central lines – and any commuter would tell you that the Northern and Central are the worst. Or British Rail, the Circle, then Central. Or take one and a half hours on two buses. If you go on the tube you arrive frazzled. It's not possible to get a seat on the Central Line when you're going out of town. It's incredibly stressful being at the behest of London Transport. I used to have a pushbike, but I came off it, and got nervous. In a car you can listen to news stations, and after an hour and a half stuck in traffic, you get a Zen-like calm and think there's no point being angry. You can get supreme superiority smiling away while everyone else is losing their rag. All this publicity about road rage just validates what people are feeling. It's made a virtue of something which should be stamped out. What all drivers need are chill-out tips.'

Chipping Camden to Birmingham

Lecturer Jill Schofield plans her commute from a village in Worcestershire to Birmingham with military skill. 'If you just go on the ordinary roads and bypass it's a seventy-four-mile round trip, but depending on what time you leave the house it can be faster to go on the motorway, which makes it a 110-mile round trip,' says Schofield. 'If I have to go in for 9 a.m. then it takes one hour and forty-five minutes to get to Birmingham. But if I start at 11 a.m. then I leave an hour. It's a big difference – and it's all because of the awful, congested M6, which always seems especially bad on Mondays when people and lorries are travelling north.'

To combat the problems Schofield, 39, has armed herself with a mobile phone and negotiates new lecture timetables fiercely. 'I bought a lovely big, safe, speedy and comfortable car, an Audi 2l, for this journey. It can be frustrating being in a jam, but even if you're stationary for ten minutes you might gain an overall fifteen minutes by using the M6, so you have to think, Cost? Benefit? You have to drive strategically. But I like moving and for me the benefits of a car outweigh the drawbacks. Even when I was stuck for four hours in a terrible jam on the M25 I still felt cars were nice to look at, have fascinating engineering and are a real technical achievement for liberating people.'

Arundel to Littlehampton, Sussex

Debbie Budden, 29, doesn't feel her five-mile journey to the Body Shop's head office is that painful – if she drives. 'I could go by train but it's a fifteen-minute walk to the station and then at Littlehampton another twenty-five-minute walk to the office. That's fine if it's nice weather, but it's not always practical and it's not door-to-door like driving.

'One of the problems is that there are two main sites at work, and sometimes I need to go from one site to another several times a day. It takes a couple of minutes to drive to them, but they are a fifteen-minute walk apart along the very busy A259. The pavement is very uneven and quite narrow in places and you're right against the road, which is very noisy, polluted and busy. Once I had to wait fifteen minutes before I could walk across the road . . . The company has just started trialling a minibus to run between the two sites but it's taking time for people to start using it.

'Some people bike to work, but for me cycling isn't an option as the road is very busy (there's a dual carriageway and several roundabouts to contend with) and there are no cycle lanes. I have two cars, one's a restored Beetle which I use when it's sunny; the other is my battered runaround, a Datsun. I find it really hard to know what would be best environmentally. The

Datsun is a cheap car to run, and though it's old I'm reusing it – surely it uses less energy if you keep an old car going? But then I think that if I could afford a new car, like Ford's Ka, then it would be good for parking, economical to run and the fuel consumption would be lower too.'

Environment city

Weaning people off their dependency on cars is futile when there are no other methods of transport. For example, although the Body Shop's head office has anti-motoring slogans painted in the car park offering a sharp reminder about the madness of motoring – AUTOMOBILE: *n*: A FOUR-WHEELED VEHICLE THAT RUNS UP BILLS AND DOWN PEDESTRIANS; GLOBAL WARNING: DRIVING CARS CAUSES 1/5 OF ALL AIR POLLUTION AND SEVERE LIFE-THREATENING CLIMATE CHANGE; as well as the more positive message from wit H. G. Wells, WHEN I SEE AN ADULT ON A BICYCLE I HAVE HOPE FOR THE HUMAN RACE – these are usually obscured by vehicles.

The one exception is on National Car Free Day, held in June. For the event in 1997 the company encouraged people to walk, cycle or car-share to work, but above all to avoid driving in on their own. Those that did were asked to pay a voluntary fine, which raised nearly £1000. But for some, getting to work without a car required Herculean effort: one man cycled thirty-four miles.

Because not everybody wants to drive everywhere – and this includes those without driving licences (like schoolkids and the very old) or those without access to a vehicle – some councils, like Leicester, have started to develop alternatives for getting around.

Leicestershire had a head start in the environmental stakes –

after all it was at the 1485 Battle of Bosworth that
Shakespeare's Richard III memorably pleaded for Green transport with the line: 'A horse, a horse, my kingdom for a horse.'
However, it wasn't until 1990 that Leicester started calling
itself Britain's first 'environment city' – and, to be fair, with
thirteen city nature reserves, sixty-five recycling bin sites, fifty
kilometres of cycle routes and the Greenest Premier Division
football ground in the country, it still has few competitors,
though Leeds, Middlesbrough and Peterborough are giving it a
run for its Green title.

Yet even in environmentally conscious Leicester most
commuters drive to work. And just like the rest of Britain it's a
city where car ownership is on the increase. This is in sharp
contrast to Continental trends – both Germany and the
Netherlands have higher levels of car ownership but people
consciously choose to walk, cycle or use public transport for
short journeys.[5]

Statistics show that more than 40 per cent of UK car journeys
are under two miles, so the Leicester-based charity Environ
decided to find out which took longer: two miles around the city
by bike or by car. The results of the road test revealed it wasn't
quicker by car. To prove this to the public a three-mile
commuter challenge, between a car, a bike, a bus passenger and
a runner, was held in April 1997. The cyclist won easily,
managing to zip down the main roads from Birstall and secure
his bike safely by Leicester Town Hall in just thirteen minutes.
The runner took eighteen minutes and the bus passenger
nineteen minutes. The car driver came last – finally finding a
parking place in the multi-storey car park after twenty-one
minutes.[6]

Yes, joggers can beat cars. Are you listening, Henry Ford?
We're programmed to believe cars are fast, but it's clear that at

certain times (like when you most want to use them) this is no longer the case. 'We didn't think the driver would win, but it was brilliant it came last,' admits Les Newby who helped organize the race. 'Of course, if it *had* won we would have said that Leicester needed to improve conditions for cyclists and bus passengers.'

A month later a government report revealed that cycling is also the fastest way of getting around London. And it's been that way for the past three years – bus, rail, tube, private-car or taxi journeys all take longer. Trips of less than four miles into the centre of London take cyclists an average thirty-four minutes; car (including a search for a space allowing at least four hours' parking) and rail trips take forty-five minutes, and the bus a dismal one hour and four minutes.[7] On journeys of more than one and a half miles in central London, cyclists took an average eighteen minutes while trains took thirty-one, cars thirty-three and bus passengers thirty-eight minutes.[8]

Wheel world ironies

Cycling is not without its problems. 'If you leave any bike on the street, locked or not, it will get nicked one day, that's guaranteed,' says Julian Wall who set up Britain's first bike park with his business partner Philip Cavell back in 1994. The idea of providing a secure site for bikes in central London was partly inspired because the friends lived in Hackney. 'There's no good public transport into the centre, so if you want to go to the cinema you can take a bus, which is very slow. Or you can drive, which is quicker – but then you spend about forty minutes looking for a space and have to pay around seven quid,' says Julian, who switches between mountain bikes and a Peugeot 106.

Bikepark is busy enough to employ about a dozen staff, but its owners are well aware that even with fifty regular users of the service the profit from just the bike-parking facility is negligible. And how could it be otherwise, at 50p for four hours, £1 for eight hours and £2 for 24 hours? 'It's not like the NCP,' explains thirty-three-year-old Julian: 'we can't make

---

Starting young

Nine-year-old Sam is a car *aficionado*. Already he understands that though all men start equal, with the aid of a good-looking set of wheels they jump places on the social grid.

At five he knew how to spell Lamborghini. Over pizza in the King's Road he monopolized all conversation by naming the type, manufacturer and year of every souped-up model passing the window of the restaurant. His ambition is to own a McLaren F1 – currently the most expensive car on the road. But despite his enthusiasm for cars Sam has cycled from London to Brighton, for charity, several times. He is one of the few kids to ride his bike to school. He's even been on a Critical Mass rally, the monthly Friday-evening ride by urban cyclists world-wide, in London where he delighted the other cyclists by shouting at a particularly desirable convertible stuck in the Trafalgar Square traffic: 'Nice car, but you can get a better bike with the money!' With experiences like this it is possible that Sam may become exactly the sort of driver our crowded roads need: someone who understands which wheels are best for which job.

our money from parking, so we need to sell bikes as well. This means that you can only have a bike park where there's a bike shop. That way you can offer parking, repairs, rentals, bikes and accessories.' It also means normal shop hours – Bikepark shuts at 7.30 p.m. – so the only cycling moviegoers who can benefit are the ones willing to see an afternoon show.

However, the Borough of Kensington and Chelsea has been so impressed by the concept as a way of encouraging office workers to leave their cars at home that it has provided some backing for Bikepark 2. The new site is on the King's Road and boasts parking for more than 150 bikes as well as showers, toilets, lockers, drying rooms and a workshop.

Julian reckons there's demand for more bike parks in London – but is still amazed by most councils' lack of interest. 'Unless the rent is dirt cheap – which is unlikely as bike parks need to be in commercial areas, ideally three or four minutes from where people work – it's a service that has to be subsidized, either by government or local authorities. We got help from Raleigh for the first one,' says Julian. But the lease is nearly up in Covent Garden and the building looks set to be turned into a residential office block. 'Where we are now will become a car park – and if they don't knock down the building, with the pillars the way they are set means only three cars will fit in here.' He leans back in his tatty office chair, narrowly missing the rows of bikes hung behind him. There's a big, tired grin on his face as he counts the number of bikes in the shop – more than a hundred. 'It's ironic, isn't it?' he says at last. 'We're offering a unique facility. For three years it's been the only bike park in London but Camden doesn't seem to care at all about the kudos – and now they're going to approve it as a car-parking space.'

Green commuter plans

One way to help people make journeys to work without relying on the car is for companies to encourage Green commuter plans, discouraging employees from driving to work alone. The idea is backed by business and government. Minister of Transport Gavin Strang MP is on record saying: 'I believe it is imperative that we reduce our dependency on the car. That is an objective to which this government is firmly committed. However, it is not something that government can – or should – achieve on its own. We have shared aspirations, we also need shared actions. Green commuter plans are one way in which organisations of all sizes, and in all sectors, can make a valuable and cost-effective contribution to achieving our aspirations.'[9]

Perhaps the most innovative Green commuting scheme is run for staff and students at Washington University in Seattle, in a bid to keep traffic levels to and from the campus at 1983 levels. Trips by car were cut by around 20 per cent after the U-Pass was introduced. The pass costs $27 for three months but allows the holder to travel free on two bus networks at any time throughout the region. At certain times (usually winter nights) these buses provide a door-to-door service. Better still, bikes are able to be taken on buses. U-Pass also allows car sharers to park free on the campus and provides access to subsidized van-pooling and a park-and-ride service.[10]

There are myriad efforts to encourage Green commuting in the UK too, and not just on National Car Free Day in June. Some organizations even reimburse staff who use their bikes for company business: the top mileage rate is paid by Southampton University Hospital (55p a mile) whilst other high payers include the University of Brighton (50p a mile), New Forest District Council (31.7p a mile) and Ipswich

Borough Council (30p a mile). Even MPs expect a cycle allowance to be introduced soon.[11]

Unfortunately, many companies are still finding it hard to get people to change a lifetime of freedom behind the wheel. Three-quarters of large companies now offer cash payments as an alternative to taking a company car, but only a handful (10 per cent) take that cash.[12] And until the tax system changes that's how it's going to stay.

Plymouth Hospitals Trust, Plymouth

As Plymouth Hospitals Trust has centralized at a site four miles from the city centre, the car parks surrounding it have had to grow fast to cater for almost four thousand staff, voluntary and contract workers making three million car trips a year. Matters came to a head when the hospital applied for extra parking space for 630 vehicles to support its latest extension, but was turned down by Plymouth City Council. 'They were acting in line with government strategy [PP13] and asked the hospital to reduce demand,' says press officer Terry West, 'but making changes to reduce pressure on existing spaces has received a mixed reception from staff – including bad feeling.'

Despite this the hospital has helped provide a range of incentives to get staff out of their cars – other than a desultory 20p all-day parking charge. A car-sharing scheme was introduced and now at least 164 staff are involved. An interest-free loan is available for the purchase of cycles or motor cycles, up to £500; a monthly newsletter helps keep all staff up to date with transport initiatives; two locked cycle sheds have been built at the hospital; there is a subsidized bus pass, which can be used seven days a week, and the local bus companies have rerouted a number of services. 'We may be the biggest car park in Devon,' says West, 'but we now have the second biggest bus terminal in

Plymouth.' But the headache continues. 'Staff do not want to see the hospital ringed with car parks; we all know that cars have an effect on our health, but discouraging people from driving to work continues to be a problem.'

Boots the Chemist, Nottingham

Around 6500 people work at Boots' head office. However, until two years ago there was no corporate commuting help. After a survey of travel styles, the commuter planning goal is to reduce traffic by 10 per cent and increase the use of buses and bikes. Already six hundred people are registered car-share users and it is hoped that this will grow to 1800. There are now sixty-eight buses a day coming to the site from surrounding areas, which has helped reduce car use. Other initiatives include a free bus link to the railway station; new lockers, showers and bike sheds to encourage cycling as well as a biannual visit from a 'bike doctor' to help fix people's bikes and free visits from the police for bike security tagging.

Thames Water, Swindon

Six years after introducing a free bus service from Swindon Station to Thames Water's new customer centre at Kembury Park, the company decided to offer something similar for its Swindon-based staff. Since 1996 two double-deckers make six trips morning and night around arranged pick-up points in Swindon, attracting around 140 people each way. The buses also provide a free service into the town centre at lunchtimes, used by at least two hundred people daily, including staff who drive to work and other people working at the industrial site. 'The service was partly offered for Green considerations, but it's cost-effective too,' said a spokeswoman, 'as it means we don't have to rent more car-parking spaces.'

Get off the road

Wandsworth-based brewers Young's was forced to call time on a centuries-old tradition of delivering beer to London pubs in horse-drawn wagons in June 1997 because of incessant complaints from impatient and intolerant motorists. Some used their mobiles to make instant complaints; the worst actually rammed into the dray.[13] Ironically, London's average daytime road traffic speed is the same now as it was back in the horse-drawn 1890s – around 10–11mph.[14] And whatever people say about mountains of smelly horse shit covering the Victorian streets, at least it was good for the roses. Particulates from our cars' exhausts are not.

Hewlett Packard, Bristol

At Hewlett Packard's offices five miles north of Bristol, all 1500 staff have the opportunity to car-share. 'It's been done in a small way though,' says environmental specialist Simon Forsyth. 'Most of the impetus has come from individual employees. First we tried a paper system, just pinning phone numbers on noticeboards, but though it was fine in principle, it was difficult to keep up to date. Then we tried a software database but it wasn't developed enough. But after a survey in 1995 we discovered that lots of people were ride-sharing informally – 43 per cent occasionally and 28 per cent regularly a few times a month. So now we help link up new starters with a car-share page of names, postcodes and internal phone numbers on the company's intranet.' The company also provides facilities for cyclists, including state-of-the-art sheds, lockers and showers, and has improved access to the nearby University of the West of England's bus terminus.

* * *

Even car companies are facing up to more flexible ways of using cars. For example, Nick Reilley, Vauxhall's managing director, says: 'The company believes that working from home, car-sharing and the use of public transport should be sensible and practical ways of addressing the problems caused by congestion.'[15] Already it has launched a congestion challenge policy.

Meanwhile, airports are beginning to invest in bus lanes – the trailblazer is on the M4. This motorway bus lane was opened at the end of September 1997 and is due to carry thirty-seven thousand bus and coach passengers a day, more than one hundred an hour, to Heathrow. Even on the first day three lanes of stationary traffic looked on enviously.

The M4 lane left BAA, formerly the British Airports Authority, with a bill of £1 million for widening the carriageway and narrowing the hard shoulder and other lanes. BAA felt it was worth it, to get the number of passengers travelling to Heathrow on public transport from 35 to 50 per cent by 2002.[16] It has also stumped up £600 million for a new rail service, the Heathrow Express, a fifteen-minute Heathrow to central London service, expected to take three thousand cars a day off the road.

BAA boss Des Wilson, who helped ensure that lead was taken out of petrol through his work with the Campaign for Lead Free Air and as chair for Friends of the Earth during the mid-1980s, is well known for his convictions about commuting. 'I don't want to be fretting in traffic jams, and I don't want the nightmare of finding and paying for parking. I want to read my newspaper on the train, knowing it will get me to where I have to be on time.' However, he points out that though 'there are countless small schemes that will help a little, when you cut through the complexities of transport policy one thing stands out a mile: someone has got to invest a lot of money in public transport and public infrastructure – the sooner that's acknowledged the sooner the full potential of public–private partnership can be achieved.'[17]

Liquid inspiration

The three o'clock coach out of Oxford has the usual mix of students and tourists, but there's also a scattering of besuited men and women doing deals on their mobiles. It's not such a surprise to see professionals here: Oxford has one train an hour to London, but a choice of at least six luxury buses – and more during peak travel times for Oxford's commuters. There's such a demand that there's even a twenty-four-hour coach service, with buses also running to the capital on Christmas Day.

At Richard Warwick and Carl Kiddell's Bromley-based office, which specializes in oil and shipping, it's normal practice to use public transport to get to meetings. Staff take the train to Hull and the coach to Oxford. Both drive, and their travel choice generally has little to do with environmental issues.

I'm aware that people driving around in cars isn't good for the environment,' says Warwick, but his motivation for taking this bus is more one of avoiding being trapped in a car all day. 'Public transport is more relaxing if you go any distance. You can read and work – though I prefer the train,' he says as the bus slows for the roadworks on the M40, just past High Wycombe.

'It made sense travelling by coach today,' adds his colleague. 'This way we didn't have to come in two separate cars. We could chat on the bus – and have a few drinks at lunchtime.'

Let's share

Another solution for today's commuter is a car-share scheme. It's an idea which makes sense, as most private cars are used for just one hour a day – yet without access to car-shares people feel obliged to buy their own vehicle, even if it spends most of its time locked up and immobile. As Edinburgh's City Car Club blurb points out, few people would buy a tennis court if they wanted to play one game, they'd just book a court from the local sports centre. Many households already share their car, but, just as people find when sharing with neighbours in an informal way, problems arise when several people need to use the car at the same time. Instead of buying a car some people rent, but the service is generally expensive and inflexible. That's why there is growing interest in joining pay-as-you-drive car-shares. The fastest growth of these clubs has been in Germany, where they are called Stadt Auto. Typically twelve households can share one car – but to ensure there isn't a run on a vehicle the clubs keep several in easy-to-reach sites. Membership in Berlin has now been taken up by more than three thousand people, and there are city car clubs operating in more than 250 European towns.

For anyone who drives less than six thousand miles a year, membership of a car-share club produces substantial cost savings as rates typically vary between £1 and £3.50 per hour. In addition, with access to a car twenty-four hours a day, and at short notice, membership of Stadt Auto has been found to reduce ownership by up to ten private cars. Not only does the concept cut pollution by reducing prolific car ownership and use, city car clubs provide access for people on lower incomes who might not otherwise be able to afford to buy or run their own car.

'The long-term environmental benefits are diverse,' claims the influential *Green Futures* magazine. 'Many fewer cars would be needed. In most Western countries today, it is obvious that the number of cars in use at any particular time, even during peak hours, is vastly outnumbered by the number of cars standing idle. A flexible car-share scheme, adopted nationally, could reduce the aggregate resource impact of the nation's private car fleet as well as saving space in crowded inner cities.'[18]

Inspired by the successes of car-sharing in Europe, Edinburgh is to have its own city car club from spring 1998 in the Marchmont/Sciennes area. 'The idea is taken from a German-Swiss model,' says John Saunders from City of Edinburgh Council, 'and will be like a car hire, but on a local neighbourhood basis. People who have joined will be able to phone the booking office, be allocated a free car and then pick it up using an electronic smart card.'

Edinburgh has high hopes for the car-share concept, believing that it can be self-financing and that because drivers pay for the amount they use the car it helps cut down on unnecessary journeys. 'For former car owners it can reduce car use by 50 per cent, just stopping people from jumping into the car to go a hundred yards down the road when they could walk or bike,' says Saunders. 'It's ideal for people living in the centre of the city, especially in high-density flats where there are major parking problems.' Such schemes may lead to a change in the attitude of the car-rental companies. Already in Tokyo it is possible to rent cars by the hour.[19]

Yet even when changes are made things can go wrong. For example, in California attempts to cut car use by rewarding drivers who fill up their car with passengers have backfired by turning everyone into a scheming lawbreaker. Most San Francisco highways have three or four lanes, but during rush hours the lane with giant white diamonds painted on it can only be used by cars with at least three people. Despite this drivers can't resist using the diamond lane, though few enjoy getting caught by police who dish out hefty fines for 'moving violations', which jack up their car insurance premiums. Excuses range from the bizarre – one pregnant woman insisted that her unborn baby counted as a commuter (a claim backed by pro-life groups) – to the weird, such as the use of blow-up dummies strapped into the back seat. A more acceptable car-filling trick for a fast commute into San Francisco is to pick up passengers waiting at out-of-town bus stops. There are also car and van pools, many for members only, which guarantee collection from a set point every morning.

Les Newby has spent the past two years in Leicester working on sustainable transport policies and Local Agenda 21 planning,[20] the process of sustainable development created by practical local action which was started at the 1992 Rio Earth Summit. He's acutely aware that the big issues locally are transport and crime. People are fed up with fumes, congestion, poor public transport, unsafe cycle routes and cars taking priority over pedestrians. At Environ, which is working in partnership with the council, a long-term vision for the city has been fleshed out which makes reducing levels of traffic, at the same time as improving public transport, the top priority. There are also proposals for the short term, to help reduce the need to drive to places like the doctor's surgery, shops or the library.

However, car-pooling hasn't taken off in Leicester. 'The problem is flexibility. Car-shares and car-pools are hard to organize,' says Newby. 'But if you look at the real reasons they don't work it's more to do with psychology. No one wants to share cars with a stranger, or someone they don't like. However, people who've seen information about car-pools are twice as likely to share journeys as those who haven't. It seems that their imagination is prompted and so they may start to share journeys informally with someone they already know, like a friend or work colleague. This is particularly the case at a workplace, where people already have a unifying factor, even if it's just the name on their pay cheque.'

Even with successes in the UK like the Road Traffic Reduction Bill 1998, changing mindsets can be notoriously hard. Local authorities are cash-strapped and government can be easily swayed by ear-bending from the roads lobby, as the *Economist* pointed out in July 1997. 'Although it is too early to write off the government's claims to greenery, the signs are not promising. Ministers seem reluctant to do anything that threatens Britons' love affair with their cars, let alone challenge the considerable vested interests behind the road lobby.'[21]

It is the dehumanizing effect of exponential growth in car ownership – the way it makes streets off-limits for kids, an unpleasant place for people to stop and socialize – which the architect, and outspoken promoter of close-knit communities, local shops and public transport, Harley Sherlock, criticizes. In his book *Cities Are Good For Us* Sherlock tracks the history of cities and puzzles why the signs that mass private car owner- ship were set to decivilize our cities were ignored.[22]

'Planners and politicians should take the blame,' he says when we meet at his office, near the hurly-burly of Farringdon Road in London. 'The Buchanan Report, published back in 1963,[23] makes clear that, for our cities to work, we can either completely rebuild the central areas – thus accommodating moving vehicles, parked vehicles and pedestrians on three different levels (rather like the Barbican) – or we can give priority to buses and delivery vehicles by imposing draconian traffic restraint.

'Buchanan was pro-car, but all he did was his sums,' continues Sherlock. 'More worryingly, he also worked out that if we all used our cars to get to work in a city, like Leeds, even if it had been rebuilt on three different levels, it couldn't keep the traffic flowing . . . In the end no policy was put in place and traffic has been left to restrain itself by its own congestion.

'Drivers know they are destroying the environment and polluting the atmosphere, but what they don't seem to realize is that cars aren't working. People assume you have to have a car for mobility, but in urban areas, like central London or Edinburgh, it's more difficult to get round in a hurry than it was thirty years ago. So we have a situation where we spend more time travelling – even though the car was invented with the idea of saving time. If all we're doing by travelling more in our cars is living at Orpington, working at Heathrow and sitting in a traffic jam on the M25 every day, that isn't progress.'

His solutions are to tackle urban housing, sort out public transport and make road travel pay its way. On paper such solutions sound simple, but without a central body taking a long-term management overview they may never be cracked. 'There's an awful long way to go,' says Sherlock. 'It could get to the stage where driving cars through cities is seen as an anti-social thing to be doing. Yes, a lot of people already think that way, but to win over the majority, as we have on smoking, is going to be hard. After all, there's even more vested interests in the oil and motor industry than in the tobacco business. For some countries it's their livelihood.'

Driving us all off road

That's why it's not just developed countries, like the UK and US, which suffer from road-driven city-planning. This is what happened to Mexico City, according to writer Ivan Illich: 'What a difference there was between the old and new parts of Mexico City (in the 1950s). In the old parts of the city, the streets were still true commons. Some people sat on the road to sell vegetables and charcoal. Others put their chairs on the road to sell tequila. Others held their meetings on the road to decide on the new headman for the neighbourhood or to determine the price of a donkey . . . Children played in the gutter, and still people walking could use the road to get from one place to another . . . The street itself was the result of people living there and making the space liveable . . . In the new sections of Mexico City, streets are no more for people. They are nowadays for automobiles, for buses, for cars, for taxis and trucks. People are barely tolerated on the streets unless they are on their way to a bus stop. If people now sat down or stopped on the street they would become obstacles for the traffic, and traffic would be dangerous to them. The road has been degraded from a commons to a simple resource for the circulation of vehicles.'[24]

One solution, banning all cars in the city centre permanently, is a radical option which few British town councils have dared suggest. And councils, desperate to attract investment, tend to resist any traffic restraints. It is only with bitter reluctance that Edinburgh has managed to claw back one lane along its main shopping parade, Princes Street, in an attempt to slash pollution and stop pedestrian shoppers getting injured.

Cambridge came close to charging car drivers for visits during peak times, before backing down. Even York, which already has fifty miles of cycleways, the highest level of bike usage in Britain, and a fifth of all residential streets traffic-calmed, still allows traffic into the centre for free. There were plans to charge drivers £1 a day to enter the city during peak periods – which could have raised £2.7 million a year – back in

April 1996. However, the idea was ditched, not just because it would discriminate against the poor, but because there were fears from traders that many out-of-town shoppers would drive to Hull or Leeds instead.[25]

Leicester Council might also have been tempted to price cars out of its centre if it didn't fear shoppers would immediately switch to Fosse Park shopping centre (with its 1650 car-parking spaces at Junction 21 of the M1), Nottingham or Derby. However, the city *was* the first in Britain to trial a smart-card system to see whether drivers would change ingrained ways of reaching work if they were charged to use the road.[26] Results showed they'd pay considerable sums rather than leave the car at home.

Oxford's rickshaw wallah

After a trip to Delhi, Erica Steinhauer decided that a British-based rickshaw company could both benefit rickshaw makers in India and provide a clean form of sustainable transport in her home town. But it took four years to persuade Oxford City Council that a fleet of pedal-powered rickshaws would be beneficial to the historic city. Despite the time lag, there are now fourteen rickshaws working the city, from a base outside Balliol College.

However, because of the Hackney Carriage Licence Act pedal-powered vehicles are not allowed to operate as roving taxis – despite their role in cities as diverse as Calcutta and Dakar – instead they can be used for pre-booked tours or to follow a set route around the city.

The British Rickshaw Network is at 40 Cowley Road, Oxford, OX4 1HZ (01865 251620, fax 01865 251134).

CHAPTER FOUR

Open road

Transport problems have been with us since the first Roman road – indeed, Julius Caesar banned wheeled transport from Rome during the daytime back in the first century BC. But since the invention of the internal combustion engine arguments between car lovers and haters have raged without pause. A prototype Disgusted of Tunbridge Wells complained in 1909: 'Wandering machines, travelling with an incredible rate of speed, scramble and smash and shriek along all the rural ways. You can see them on a Sunday afternoon, piled 20 or 30 deep outside the new popular inns, while their occupants regale themselves within. You can see evidence of their activity in the dust-laden hedges of the south country roads, a grey mud colour, with no evidence of green; in the ruined cottage gardens of the south country villages.'[1]

Fell walker and author Alfred J. Brown denounced cars with similar vitriol in 1928, raging: 'This little land of ours is beset by a hideous invader; a ubiquitous Thing on Wheels of multiple forms, but of one devouring purpose, which is to eat up our very roads, to tear up our very byways, to massacre our few remaining Shanks' Mares, to choke the last Guard of the old legion of Walkers, to throw dust in their eyes, to set traps for their legs, and, in a word, to knock them down and exterminate them utterly.'[2] The same year architect Clough Williams-Ellis, creator of what's become known as *The Prisoner*'s village, Portmeirion in Wales, warned that the countryside was being wrecked by tarmac roads.[3]

Same old record?

Things used to be better – at least that's what the older generation always seem to say. One of Britain's oldest people, Vincent Gulliver, told an interviewer on his 109th birthday that he was tired of the changes brought during the twentieth century. 'When I was young there were no cars or buses on the road, and not half so much trouble either. I despair at today's new-fangled society.'

Gulliver was born in November 1887 – the same month that Queen Victoria celebrated her golden jubilee – and ten years before the horseless carriage would roll out of Coventry. He died in August 1997, but the jury is still deliberating about whether society should rejoice or despair at the invention of the motor car.[4]

It was the pointlessness of excessive road-building which angered Lord Kennet, speaking in the House of Lords about the impact of the Newbury Bypass on the River Kennet floodplain, in 1996. He felt that those with eyes to see should try looking: 'My Lords, should not the Prime Minister witness the death throes of an impossible transport policy – hundreds of policemen, private security men and bailiffs, trying by force to evict the people who have chosen to camp in the friendly trees to protect them, and the gigantic machines waiting to uproot the trees, all in favour of juggernauts carrying nothing more important than frozen food from another country.'[5]

Almost all our beautiful places now suffer from too many vehicles, making them considerably less beautiful. Of the 154.4 million trips of one night or more away from home each year, around 80 per cent are made by car.[6] As a result, front lawns become an off-road parking bay and traffic signs start to clutter country lanes whilst the picture-postcard villages of rural Britain and our historic cities turn into dirty, dusty, noisy, polluted jams and car parks. Yes, you *can* still escape from the smoke, but for how long?

Holidaying hell

Roy Preston lives in the centre of Christchurch, Dorset, in a street which is used by 1200 vehicles and up to forty buses an hour. 'The road was only created for carthorses. It's got two Grade I listed bridges yet it's used as a rat run, leaving the atmosphere of the town nothing more than diesel and petrol exhaust,' he says, 'and in the summer it is terrible. Traffic management is so behind here. We have forty-eight thousand people and all we've got is one pedestrian crossing in the whole mile of the conservation-area rat run.'

So, putting his graphic-design training to use he created Jenny and her family, tourists who'd come to Christchurch, and made them write postcards, one every two days, to the local councillors, showing scenes of a less than pleasant traffic-cramped town. The aim was to prick consciences and make people laugh, wondering about how their town had turned from a picture postcard into a polluted jam. The pictorial strike was followed by a surprise package for every councillor: a spray bottle containing the fragrant new perfume L'Air de

Christchurch. 'They thought I was a terrorist at first! There were even rumours that I was sending out petrol bombs – but it was just a touch of diesel,' says Preston with a laugh, 'and though there was really nice packaging, it did have a warning: "Caution, contents carcinogenic."'

Preston's postcard campaign was followed by the region's media and already a public seminar has been held to enable local groups to present ideas about what they think ought to be done to clean up the town. 'I've tried not to attack the council, that's why the postcards were used. The idea is to be a friendly enemy and help them see how ridiculous it is when the car is treated with more importance than people.'

Leaning on our cars

But cars get us to work, to the shops, to visit friends and family, and out of the house for all sorts of sport and leisure activities. They are used to tryst, to drive the kids to school, to get to the gym and to dump bottles, cans and newspapers at the recycling centre. Cars have become so indispensable, especially for people living in the countryside, that some families end up having as many cars as drivers.[*]

Can't do without them

The Rawsons are just one of the millions of British multi-car families. They live in Hertfordshire, a county with one of the highest numbers of cars per head. Their home is a hilly two miles from the nearest bus stop and three from the nearest shop. Dad is a doctor and needs a car to get to the surgery and make

[*]*The Car, the Environment and the Economy* (RMI, June 1997) calculates that 68 per cent of all households now have a car, and of those, 23 per cent have more than one. In rural areas 70 per cent of households have a car.

Modern madness

Robert Davis is a transport consultant with a passion for bikes. For years Davis has been anticipating a crackdown on car use, and for years he's been disappointed. 'The place to do it is in the country,' he says. 'I cycle past the beautiful houses in the villages of east Hertfordshire, places like Much Hadham, and wonder who could want to live there. Cars are racing past all the time, and as it's such a commuter belt this goes on even at night. Isn't the point of the country that you want peace and quiet? It's rural areas where cars are doing the damage and there is an inability by car owners to accept responsibility.'

Hertfordshire has one of the highest car-owning populations in Britain, but it wasn't always that way. Davis remembers tales from his uncle, who used to motor down from London for the occasional weekend at a time when locals rarely travelled further than the distance they could walk from their home. 'He hardly ever passed a car,' recalls Davis, 'but it's not just pre-war changes, there's been a huge change over the past thirty years. Many of the people living in that area think it's madness to walk, cycle or ride a horse along those country lanes now. They think it's just too hazardous.'

Copies of Davis's book Death on the Streets: Cars and the Mythology of Road Safety *(Leading Edge, 1993) available from Road Danger Reduction Forum, PO Box 2944, London NW10 2AX.*

house calls. As his Polo is out all day his wife also needs a car so she's not trapped at home. Mostly she uses it for shopping and to get to her part-time job. Their three kids live at home, and all have cars. Joy uses hers to drive to the station (thirty minutes) and then commute by train up to London (forty minutes). Annie has a Peugeot 205, without which she wouldn't be able to keep her part-time job in a nearby village. The youngest, Andrew, is at sixth form in nearby Bishop's Stortford. Recently he was handed the keys to an eight-year-old Mini, after the family found they had a 'spare car' following the death of a relation. This means he can drive himself to college – giving both his parents more flexible diaries. 'Having so many vehicles is selfish and uneconomical and causes more pollution,' admits Dr Rawson, who recently expanded his driveway to ensure all the vehicles had parking space, 'but because we live in the countryside, and are often all in different places, we are dependent on our cars.'

Catch-22

Peter Brock, research fellow at Exeter University's Centre for Energy and the Environment, spends his work hours considering alternatives to the car. But even he is wedded to his Peugeot 205. 'Having a car is a fantastic liberator. I'm well aware of the damage it is causing, and I make conscious efforts to limit my use. But I still use it in an unsustainable way. Even when people are aware of the problem it's difficult not to be party to it. I just wish there was a simple answer. Where I live there isn't a shop around – what there were have closed because people used their cars to drive to the supermarkets – so it's a Catch-22.'

Drive 'n' Shop

Les Newby, at Environ in Leicester, thinks car-park taxation could reduce people's use of out-of-town shopping centres. 'The tax would hit the owner of the supermarket, business or car park, discouraging people from providing as much car-parking or ensuring a massive hike in parking-ticket prices. The group it would really hit would be out-of-town shopping centres, whose existence is based on oceans of free parking.'

It's a point Harley Sherlock makes too: 'One of the biggest scandals is how retailers have conned their customers by telling us that it's more convenient to get stuff from them, at the superstores. It may be cheaper, but how can it be more convenient than the stores delivering it to us or at least getting the more popular brands to corner shops close to where people live? It would be much better to have lots of mini-supermarkets in each neighbourhood, like the Tesco Metro shops, rather than one great big superstore.'

Home delivery

There are tentative experiments with home deliveries – a service which was anyway a normal part of life until the twentieth century, and which has left its legacy with the signs on big houses that point to the 'tradesmen's entrance' or stipulate 'no hawkers'. Nowadays door-to-door calls are more likely to be nappy-washing services, deli vans packed with frozen dinner-party meals, or cable TV sales. Sherlock is certain there could be a better service and is trying to persuade his local supermarket that it should take produce to the customer, rather than attract customers to a permanently chock-a-block car park, in the same way that the Next catalogue or any mail-order system operates.

Already there are a number of Internet shopping experiments which enable customers to shop from the PC rigged up in their sitting room. Tesco began its home shopping service in 1996 for people living in Romford, Essex, Osterley, Middlesex, Hammersmith and Lea Valley, London, Sutton, Surrey, and Leeds. They can order via the Net, fax or phone. It's a service that has proved popular enough to extend to four new areas already. The older generation, who remember door-to-door deliveries, must find Tesco's suggestion 'What can be more convenient than having all your regular groceries, including fresh fruit and vegetables or that special bottle of wine delivered to your doorstep?' slightly disingenuous. After all, it's the superstores that have led to the disappearance of so many of our local shops and delivery services.

Trolley good

It's all rather confusing – wasn't the one-stop shop at the superstore meant to be convenient too, until we found our cars converted into little more than luxury shopping trolleys? Indeed Tesco, perhaps fed up with endless complaints about their unmanageable trolleys, have managed to outmanoeuvre the most vocal critics with the launch of the 225 Mk X11 – a new trolley. Jeremy Clarkson road-tested it, and the result was history: 'I've always described bad cars as handling like a supermarket trolley. That's what I'm going to say about good cars in the future. This is an end to trolley rage – which is a shame – but at least you can speed in it. I think they've concentrated on handling more than styling. The only basic problem is the engine, which is knackered, old, two-cylinder me. We're going to have to find a whole new use for trolley metaphors.'[7]

The question is, will supermarkets fight back against any disenchantment with the car? Tesco, with 588 stores (and growing) and twelve million customer transactions a week (or 636 million a year) seems to be adapting, slowly. It now has thirty-six non-super stores – they are the Tesco Metros, which began to appear in town and city centres after the first one proved such a success in Covent Garden when it was opened in 1992.

Tesco's rival for the family shopping, Sainsbury's, which has 378 stores and around twelve and a half million customers a week, is also trialling new shopping techniques. After a successful experiment at Solihull, the first remote shopping scheme was introduced at Watford and is due to be introduced to a dozen more stores soon. At Watford around three hundred customers, mostly women, have a personal shopping catalogue at the store. When they need goods they phone or fax over an order which is put together by Sainsbury's team of personal shoppers. The customer then picks up the order at a pre-arranged time. Though this system saves time, it doesn't cut down on traffic. However, Sainsbury's other food retailing group, Savacentre, does the delivering to Hewlett Packard's Bracknell headquarters for anyone shopping over the company's intranet. This system is used by around a hundred people and is due to be trialled at other stores. As so few house-holds in the UK are on the Net, Sainsbury's is cautious about electronic shopping. 'We don't believe that the Internet is the answer to most people's shopping needs, but we do know that around 20 per cent of our customers are interested in some form of remote shopping,' says a Sainsbury's spokesman. This may lead to a surge in television shopping channels – Sainsbury's is currently talking with BSkyB about possibilities.

At Iceland, which has three million customers a week at its 770 stores, the thinking is very different, precisely because of their high-street locations. The company began a free home delivery service for anyone spending £25 or more in March 1997, after trialling the concept in Scotland. 'We identified that over 65 per cent of our customers do not have access to a car during the day,' said Barbara Crampton, a spokeswoman for Iceland. It's a service which makes sense for everyone: workers can shop in their lunch hour, knowing their goods will be delivered in the evening, it also saves the elderly, infirm and mothers with young children from the trial of carrying. 'It also means you can do the shopping anytime, you don't have to think, Well that's frozen so I'll have to buy it last,' adds Crampton. The store is also experimenting with home shopping in Edinburgh and the north-east, but it is doing this via a catalogue and phone – 'something everyone knows how to use,' explains Crampton. 'We feel not many people have access to the Internet or are confident enough to shop on it, contrary to the media hype.'

However, Asda, with 216 stores and 6.2 million customers a week, feels there is no need for change. 'Four years ago we found that 83 per cent of our shoppers used cars to visit our stores, with 8 per cent walking and 5 per cent using local transport. The figures show that Asda shoppers prefer to use cars, even though stores may be well served by public transport,' says a spokesperson. However, she promises that 'all new stores are designed with provision for cyclists, pedestrian access, accessibility by public transport and taxi pick-up points from free taxi phones.' Asda operates free shuttle buses at fifty-seven stores, requiring an investment of around £1 million, but points out tartly that provision of 'local services does ultimately rest with the local authorities'.

But Green campaigner Chris Ashby doesn't think the superstores' efforts amount to much. 'Supermarkets with massive car parks or the out-of-town centres destroy local shops. At the end of the day what we want are local shops which are close to where people live so you don't need to drive to them. It's not that Greens are all anti-cars – even though they knock people down, pollute the atmosphere, cause climate change, clutter up the streets and are unsustainable – it's that if we didn't have so many cars our local areas would be so much nicer. It would give people more space, there could be wider pavements, tree-lined streets and a much more healthy environment for everyone.'

Waste of space

The problem is that, whenever one car is taken off the road, another car takes up that space. For example, a hundred people in cars, travelling alone, need two thousand square metres of road space; whereas if they were travelling by bus they would use only forty square metres of road space. Driving on your own isn't just wasting space, it's also wasting energy. A car uses 1860 calories of energy per passenger mile, buses 920, trains 885, walking 100 and cycling just 35.[8] What's more, cycling is good for you.

'People in Essex are never going to cut back on the use of the car unless there are really good alternatives, especially in the rural parts,' admits Clive Bennett, chairman of the transport subcommittee of CPRE Essex.* 'That's why I'm not totally anti all cars. What people have to do is select the appropriate transport. There's no point driving into central London – and if you go by train you can get good deals travelling at off-peak times. But buses do have a bad image. If people know someone goes on a bus, they think, Poor old So-and-so, they can't afford a car.

'Everyone is in love with their cars, but the running costs for one person make them expensive – though it goes down if there

*CPRE: Council for the Protection of Rural England.

are more people in your car,' he adds. To prove this the group marked Local Transport Day in March 1996 by using different methods of transport – train, bus, by bike and foot – to get from Chelmsford to local tourist spots like Thornwood Park at Brentwood, Battlesbridge Antiques Centre and Mangapps Farm Railway Museum. The idea of getting anywhere in Essex without a car attracted so much interest that Anglia TV actually ran a report on the evening news!

'If we look at the real motoring costs, based on a rate per mile used by local government [42.1p per mile for a 1.8 litre engine] then travel by car for one person is considerable,' says Bennett. 'Car travel was double the public-transport cost if you are travelling alone or on public transport where children travel free. So it is cheaper to go by bus, and cheaper still to cycle or walk. Cars may be quick and convenient but they are expensive as well as environmentally unfriendly.'[9]

What the Essex group made clear to drivers was how driving is more expensive than people think. Yet a myth persists that driving is the cheapest form of travel. Drivers tend to forget to do their sums and ignore the high subsidies that have been poured into the road network. And they rarely count the amount of time their car just sits waiting to be used into the total sum either. As the *Economist* put it in a survey on 'Living with the Car', 'If drivers were made to pay more of the true cost of each trip, they might either travel less or use public transport, which usually causes less pollution per passenger. Either outcome, or a mixture of both, would make it easier to live with the car.'[10]

An end to anarchy

The days of total freedom for car owners to drive where they like are at an end. We'll never have it so good again. It's not just legislation that is going to bring about the death of our anarchic driving styles; it's the sheer number of cars which will soon be joining us on already crowded roads. And this is sure to be fuelled by successive governments seeking to cut pollution levels. The Henley Centre predicts the introduction of road pricing or congestion taxes in a bid to reduce demand for road travel and build on the technical advantages of working at home.[11]

The early millennium years are set to see a massive debate about intrusion and betrayal of individual civil liberties when car curbs are introduced – but the arguments may ring hollow. We've loved, cherished and abused our cars for more than a hundred years. Choking fumes, gridlock and tragic deaths are the unwanted by-products of our obsession with cars, but if we can't control the monsters of our own making, someone else is going to step in. The twenty-first century may see the end of free-market pioneer Adam Smith's invisible hand, and the beginning of invisible restraints. Look out for cars with chips which keep them to speed limits by beacon control at the side of the road. Such restraints will have to be tamper-proof – after all, it wasn't long ago that Jeremy Clarkson showed viewers of *Motor World* how to tape over the on-board computer of a 4x4 so he could hit top speeds on the roads around Abu Dhabi.

Heaven is a 4x4

From the moment they pass the ticket turnstiles into the massive Earls Court exhibition centre, any fear of falling for a woman disappears. At every stand, men – on their own; with colleagues, partners, siblings, fathers and friends; even in groups – are falling in love, truly, madly, deeply. They're doing it publicly, and they're doing it noisily. The new crop of cars modelling at the Motor Show is drooled over, patted and poked.

Leather seats are sat in, drinks holders pulled out, seat positions adjusted and boots slammed. There's talk about torque, gearing, advanced braking systems and acceleration. There are shouts of 'I'm in love!'

Amongst the stands roams the holy trinity of speed, status and good sales pitches, backed by choirs of decorative, uniformed young women offering vital statistics from gleaming brochures. Not every visitor admiring the flashy new models at the show is male, but it's the men I notice as they size up the new Peugeot 406 coupé; the violet TVR 4.5l Cerbera, which boasts speeds in excess of 180 mph (very handy for London) and carries a price tag of £46,500; the Mercedes S class, which despite Princess Diana's death is reputedly one of the safest models around; and a host of 4x4s including Land-Rover's new baby, the winsomely named Freelander.

For most visitors the Motor Show is the ultimate fantasy showroom, and it's a long, long way from Arthur Daley. For potential buyers wondering how the Isuzu Trooper shapes up in mud or the new sporty Land-Rover tackles water, there's an outdoor, off-road course. This purpose-built course of a one-foot-deep pond, gymkhana circuit and hand-painted sixteen-metre-high mountain – which allows potential buyers to look down on the jams of Warwick Road where but for the grace of God they may soon be – is the first to be erected in England. The National Exhibition Centre at Glasgow, however, trialled a similarly popular obstacle course five years ago.

Professional driver Dennis Patstone takes me round the designer's bizarre conception of country living in the new Land-Rover Discovery. The ride is so smooth that even crossing a fallen tree, driving up a ramp over a builder's skip and the forty-five-degree tilt seem rather disappointing. I'd expected a rougher ride – everyone knows you don a bra for a go in a

Land-Rover. But Patstone explains that with this model, with its
eight forward gears and two reverse (so many gears in fact that
he doesn't even need to touch the brakes as we come down the
'mountain'), the drive ought to be smooth.

The five-door model, priced around £21,890–£30,220,[12] may
be a lifestyle purchase for people hankering for off-road
challenges, but most will end up doing the school run or being
used by builders. This might be a good thing too – when these
vehicles do go off-road they have the potential to do a lot more
than plough muddy tracks along the verge of a country lane.
Today's 4x4ers use them to fly-tip on secluded bridleways,
wreck green lanes which have been designated as RUPs (road
used as path) by the county council's bridleways and footpath
officer, or create stunning crop circles during off-road police
chases.

As we discuss the Freelander's performance over a cup of
tea, one of Patstone's colleagues mutters about how 4x4s rarely
get to do anything they're capable of, other than mounting the
occasional kerb. Currently there's a craze amongst well-off
Americans for a 4x4 that even dwarfs the Range-Rover, the
Chevrolet Suburban 2500, which carries a price tag of
£40,000. More a tank than a car, the Suburban is the ultimate
off-road vehicle. It is in permanent four-wheel drive, clad in
snow tyres whatever the weather, and capable of pulling a
forty-foot yacht out of the sea. However, the typical Suburban
driver uses it just for trips to the shop – regardless of the fact
that it can accommodate nine people and guzzles fuel, doing
twelve miles to the gallon on the highway, around four in traffic.

It's being snapped up by the suburban drivers of LA for
different reasons: it's a high ride, has TV screens in the rear
rows, recycled-air options and, thanks to its armour-plating
and reinforced chassis around six inches higher than a car, it is

very safe. One writer called them 'lethally effective battering rams', but an owner put it differently: 'I love the fact that if me or my kids get hit, I'm going to survive and so are they. We're not the ones going to be crushed.'[13]

The nineteenth-century philosopher John Stuart Mill claimed that freedom was anything that does not adversely affect others. Unfortunately, our fondness for personal freedom in our cars has become a tyranny for all other road users, especially for those not in motor vehicles. As Roger Vincent at the Royal Society for Prevention of Accidents (RoSPA) warns: 'Unless people improve their driving standards they will have to have control taken away from them. People will complain about intrusion, but if people want to continue enjoying driving, as they say they do, they are going to have to be more responsible.' The only hitch is that, without a thorough shake-up of our own driving habits, it may already be too late.

CHAPTER FIVE

Fatal attraction

Even at accident blackspots, less than an hour after a crash there may be few signs of what's happened. Perhaps just a skid mark and some shards of windscreen. Then, as the news of a fatal accident passes round friends and family of the victim, people start feeling the need to do something to mark the incident. They may cry, they may break the news to others, they may pray. The angry will be seeking revenge – it's not unusual for relatives of someone who's died after colliding with a tree to take an axe or chainsaw to the offending trunk.

If the road is in a residential area, a few hours after the accident the first bouquet of flowers may appear. It will be left at the approximate site of the crash, just like the police sign appealing for witnesses. As the days pass the bouquets mount. The funeral is held. The flowers fade and die long before the inquest is held – but by then the bouquets will have been shifted to railings, a lamppost or the nearest tree, tied at breast height, becoming just another shrine to a nameless accident victim in an accident that wouldn't have happened if only . . . if only it wasn't the twentieth-century way of death.

But there are things we can do to make roads less of a killing field. After all, being a non-driver didn't stop Barbara Castle becoming Minister of Transport nor managing to introduce the breath test to catch drink drivers back in 1967.[1] It wasn't a popular move but over the past thirty years it has become totally unacceptable to have 'one for the road'.

Dying business

Since the invention of the car around twenty-five million people have died as victims of road traffic. This is approximately the same number that died in the great plagues in Europe. It is three times as many as died in World War I.[2] The figures are quoted in German author Winfried Wolf's book *The Car Society*. Wolf is angry that these deaths seem to go unnoticed. Using the World Health Organization's figures, which show that a quarter of a million people are killed on the roads world-wide each year, he concludes: 'The effects are similar to the bombs dropped on Hiroshima and Nagasaki. In the states of the European Union, in the early 1990s, around 50,000 people were killed annually on the streets . . . It is easier to predict traffic deaths than gross domestic product; we already know that in the decade to come 100,000 people will be killed on German roads and 1.5 million will be severely injured.'[3]

In Britain during 1996, 3598 people died in car crashes and 320,302 were injured – nearly all as a result of driver error.[4] During a car's lifetime there is a one in six chance that it will be involved in an accident which injures someone; a one in thirty-nine chance of someone being seriously injured; and a one in 580 chance that someone will be killed.[5] In France your chances of dying in a road accident are twice as high as in the UK; at eight thousand people, that's the equivalent of fifty large plane crashes.[6] It's even more dangerous on the roads of

Greece, Portugal, Ireland and Belgium. There's even a box to tick on the driving licence application form which asks if you would be willing to donate your organs 'after your death'. So just who is a danger on the roads?

Inexperienced and under twenty-one

Newly qualified drivers aged between seventeen and twenty-one years old make up just 10 per cent of all drivers, but cause 20 per cent of accidents. In July 1997 the driving test was revamped to include a theory paper, the biggest change since the test was introduced in 1935.[7] The tougher test reduced applications by half and left the British School of Motoring, which teaches one in six motorists to drive, with a substantial drop in profits.[8]

Old drivers as timebombs

Elderly drivers have often been seen as careful motorists, but over the past ten years the number of drivers over seventy has risen by four hundred thousand. By 2010 it is likely that elderly drivers will outnumber those under sixty. This means that tragedies like the eighty-six-year-old woman who had a heart attack at the wheel, causing her car to plough into the pavement and kill Jill Wilson, a thirty-four-year-old mother, and seriously injure her child, may become less of a rarity. The EU is currently pressing for drivers over the age of seventy to sit a driving test every two years.[9]

Always crashing in the same car

Company car drivers have 30–50 per cent more accidents a year than drivers of privately owned vehicles.[10] Already drivers have to sit a retest if they collect six penalty points within two years of gaining a full driving licence; but the EU thinks the

deal should be tougher, to force complacent motorists to kill
bad habits and curb reckless driving. There are proposals that
drivers should retake a test every ten years in a bid to stop the
annual forty-five thousand deaths on Europe's roads.[11]

Half of those killed will not be drivers. Indeed the first category
of people to die from injuries caused by cars in both the UK
and the US were pedestrians. At the inquest for Mrs Bridget
Driscoll, who was hit by a car travelling at just 4 mph at Crystal
Palace on 17 August 1896, making her the first person in Britain
to be killed by a car, the coroner said he hoped such an incident
would never happen again.[12] But it has, again and again. The
US had to wait another three years before seeing their first
pedestrian victim, Henry Bliss, who was fatally hit in New York
as he gallantly assisted a lady passenger off the bus.[13] Yet, by
1951 a million Americans had died on the roads when fifty-two-
year-old Mrs Elma Wischmeir was run over and killed.[14] It
didn't stop the demand for cars – that December, the hundred-
millionth passenger car built in the US was ready for the road.[15]

Pedal cyclists are at high risk of being hit by other vehicles,
but many cycling advocates, including doctors, point out that,
because of cycling's myriad benefits to our health and fitness,
riding a bicycle should be seen as less dangerous than not riding
a bicycle.

Many victims of the car will also be passengers. Yet journalists prefer to report the joyride gone wrong, the hit-and-run, the
minibus of kids which crashes on a school trip, the speeding
coach which overturns and the police car knocking over a
pedestrian whilst answering a 999 call. The facts show that men
have more accidents than women,[16] but not long ago the
Evening Standard reported that people's crash potential could
be read in the stars. Worst offenders were Virgo, followed by

Taurus. Scorpios seemed to be the safest drivers. The management firm which commissioned the study, Velo, which manages more than fifty thousand fleet vehicles, did however cautiously admit: 'While our statisticians are not entirely convinced that the differences are due to the movements of the planets, we cannot offer any other explanation.'[17]

Most people have direct experience of someone they know dying or being seriously injured in a crash. And though it may be tempting to think that a crash is just an accident of fate, the facts reveal a different picture. The odds are high, as the chance of dying on the roads is one in 125. Compare that to the likelihood of winning the lottery jackpot, one in fourteen million.[18] But because news reporting is about the unusual – Man Bites Dog – and because these deaths are inevitable, they rarely make the papers.

Horror speeds

Austrian Formula 1 driver Niki Lauda spent four days in intensive care after one of the sport's worst televised shunts, at Nürburgring on 1 August 1976. After the accident newspapers played on the public's horror by running headlines like, MY GOD, WHERE IS HIS FACE? In the pubs people overdosed on ghoulish one-liners, wisecracking: 'What burns better than Shell?' Amazingly, Lauda was driving thirty-three days later – and by the time he retired, in 1985, he had clocked up three world championship titles. But even though Lauda knew all about the downside of speeding, including seeing several colleagues die on the track, he revelled in being famous enough to get away with 'minor' road crimes. 'If the police pull me over for driving too fast, I have a better chance of getting away with it . . . I might say, "Sorry officer, I'm in training for the next

Grand Prix. How do you expect me to improve if I have to creep along the motorway at 70 mph?" The odds are that he will laugh and let me off the hook.'[19]

We all know that the police don't enforce speeding laws with any consistent rigour. Pulled over for speeding is not seen as a crime, more a case of bad luck. Throughout the country, if you're flashed it's less likely to be road rage than to warn of a police car ahead. Indeed the fraternal motorists' cop alert is a tradition which goes back to the early days of the AA, when the Chief Constable of Surrey, Captain Mowbray Saint, made it his job to put an end to the 'nuisance and danger caused by reckless riders and drivers'. He failed miserably, thanks to AA guile. At the time, the organization's staff saluted members they passed on the road – but if they were nearing a speed trap they simply 'forgot' to do so. Although this tradition is no longer practised, it used to be part of what the AA is still proud to call 'courtesy and care'.

Safety campaigners

Attitudes like these have led one campaign group, RoadPeace, to hit back. After finding that seven out of ten people admit to exceeding the speed limit regularly – even in urban areas – the group pointed out that Britain's speeding culture is a major cause of traffic 'accidents', many of which have fatal conse-quences.

'These deaths are not accidents,' says RoadPeace's Joanne Browning, whose five-month-old daughter, Alice, despite being strapped into a child's car seat, died after the car she was travelling in was hit head-on by another car in May 1994. The shocking part of this tragedy is that the other car's driver was fined £250 for 'careless' driving and had her licence endorsed with eight penalty points.[20] 'How can we accept this "accident" idea. Fewer than 1 per cent of road deaths and injuries are the result of a true accident, like mechanical failure; the other 99 per cent are negligence.'[21]

RoadPeace's former chairperson, Sandra Green, believes the word 'accident' is just too trivial to be used. '"Accident", in relation to a road death, should be banned from our vocabulary. It's totally insulting and trivializes the seriousness of the event,' she says. 'Behind every accidental death due to a car crash is a human being. We are the highest of evolved species and we can exercise choice whether to drink, to speed, to take risks, to be selfish and inconsiderate, even violent. These are voluntary acts, not accidental.'

Like many RoadPeace members who staff a twenty-four-hour helpline, Sandra Green lost a family-member in a road traffic collision: her son Paul was just twenty-three, and about to be married, when he was killed by a man in a vehicle 'unfit' to be on the road. The driver got a £250 fine and two penalty points. Though this was 1986, such a charge is typical of the British legal system which still ignores the consequences of dangerous driving, ensuring that someone's death is an irrelevance when it comes to passing sentence. Not surprisingly those left behind are left feeling their relative's life is worth nothing. Yet libel settlements – where no one is physically injured – can run to small fortunes.

Bereavement damage has recently been hiked up to £7,500: an amount which can probably fund the funeral, headstone and perhaps even a holiday for the traumatized family. But for families on low incomes it's a double-edged gift, causing huge problems if it tips them out of eligibility for state benefit.

'What RoadPeace wants is road-danger reduction,' adds Green. 'We're not talking about road safety. Look at the congestion and pollution that happens because it's not safe for children to walk to school. Go outside any school and you'll see parents parking all over the place, on double lines, anywhere. No one can move and they are just adding to the danger. A car is a lethal weapon, if you point it at someone and you drive into them.'

Britain already has the worst statistics for child pedestrian victims compared with other European countries. As Green points out: 'Cars cannot co-exist with the old, the young, pedestrians or anyone that can't move faster than it. When you get in a car there should be a voice which says: "You are now driving a vehicle that has the potential to kill you and other people." Since my son's been killed I say a prayer before turning the engine on.' Despite this, Green is no hater of cars. She lives in a rural part of the Midlands and points out that she'd be unable to visit friends or family without a car. What she wants are people's head-in-the-sand attitudes to change. 'I can still remember Coventry's Mayor saying: "Are you against cars? Because if that's the case, you are in the wrong place," when he was invited, along with police, accident and emergency staff and friends and families of those who had been killed, to a remembrance service,' she says. 'In the Midlands, Toyota is up the road, there's Coventry and Derby – all with strong links with the motor industry. But that service was to remember the war on our roads; people came to it from London, Bristol and Durham. The problem though is that most people think it's not going to happen to them, but it does – ten times every day.'

RoadPeace now provides a pack to help other churches run similar memorial services, on the Sunday after Remembrance Day, which has led to special services at places such as Derby, Birmingham, Stoke, London, Leeds and Hull.

'The country needs educating about what cars could, should and ought to be doing. We have the technology: why not make a vehicle entering a 20 mph zone have an on-board responder which would make the vehicle slow down if the driver isn't going to? They do it with coaches already,' adds Green. 'There could even be a day when the car reacts, not the driver – and if this saves just one human life then it's worth it. But at the moment, property is still more valuable than a human life. That's why RoadPeace believes there should be a criminal charge, death by driving.'

The trivial way a road death is regarded in law, and the lack of any statutory support in Britain, inspired Brigitte Chaudhry to set up RoadPeace in 1992, after her twenty-six-year-old son, Mansoor, was killed on his motor bike by a van driver going through a bank of twelve red traffic lights. After pleading guilty, the van driver was fined only £250 and given eight penalty points.

Germany, France, Holland, Switzerland, Belgium, Italy, Luxembourg and Greece do not have such a lax approach to road crimes. When death results from a crash they bring a charge of manslaughter, not careless driving.

Writing in the *Evening Standard* George Monbiot, UN Global Environment Award winner, pointed out the law's inadequacies in a graphic column explaining why we are all victims of the metal monster. 'Had the man who killed Tom, the five-year-old son of a friend of mine (and was fined £400 with costs), instead strode out of his house in a rage one night, and smashed a car windscreen to silence its alarm, he may well have been sent to prison. Pedestrians hitting cars is a graver offence than cars hitting pedestrians.'[22]

Even drink driving can result in a tougher sentence than killing someone. Compare the consequences of five-year-old Tom's death with the fine given to Tory MP Sir Nicholas Bonsor's son. Alexander Bonsor, twenty, was caught over the limit with eight Bristol University chums crammed into his car after watching the England v. Italy World Cup qualifier. He was fined £480 and banned for fourteen months for drink-driving. [23]

'To lose someone through a sudden, violent death is hard enough to cope with; to see those responsible getting away without any legal censure arouses feelings of deep anger and betrayal,' wrote journalist and bereaved father Roger Barry in a *Guardian* feature criticizing the government's wheeling out of another ineffective 'Speed Kills' campaign.[24]

A similar organization to RoadPeace, Brake, was set up by a bereaved daughter. First Mary Williams's mother was killed by a lorry with defective brakes in 1992, and then her motoring-journalist boyfriend died after an engineer with General Motors Europe crashed into his car on the B655, near Hitchin in Hertfordshire, in January 1997.

'If there was a disease that was killing 3600 people a year, and seriously injuring forty-five thousand, there would be a lot of money being ploughed into finding a cure,' says Williams, who is executive director of the organization. She's right: just compare the focus on Aids and HIV. 'Brake treats the road as a safety-critical working environment. If you were working in a factory on a piece of machinery that could chop your arm off, nobody would expect you to do another task at the same time, and you'd be expected to have had proper training,' says Williams.

Not surprisingly, Brake's first campaigns were focused on professional drivers, but the organization is also concerned about what happens in court. 'The jury is made up of members of the public, most of whom are drivers, and most of whom believe they are careful and competent. But they probably aren't. Yet they have to reach a decision on the defendant's driving. If you had a jury of highly trained Royal Mail drivers, they'd find most people guilty in two seconds. Bad driving is socially acceptable,' adds Williams.[25]

Even Bryan Lunn, chief examiner at the Institute of Advanced Motoring, a policeman for thirty-two years who has intimate experience of the courts and road traffic accidents, points out the ironies. 'With my police background I can understand why if there's an accident and someone is killed that doesn't enter into the court proceedings – but it doesn't make it right.'

People *do* get banned for dangerous driving, drunk driving or for driving without due care and attention. But things are getting more complicated: recently police found that more drivers are killed on the roads under the influence of drugs like cannabis than are over the drink limit. Research by Granada TV showed that most motorists aged between twenty-two and twenty-five thought drug-driving, especially on dope or speed, was common amongst their age group. The problem is that drugs are much harder to detect, although German scientists are experimenting with a skin-swipe test which could pinpoint users.[26]

Often those who are pulled up for driving without due care and attention are convinced they've done nothing wrong – some people think it's perfectly OK to check a map at 50 mph or sit in the middle lane of the motorway gassing on the mobile. It's not: but not enough people are caught and charged.

The power of speed

In *Crash*, speeding is the turn-on and crashing the ultimate thrill. J. G. Ballard may have written a hazard warning – in the introduction to the French edition (published in 1974) he wrote that the book's 'ultimate role . . . is cautionary, a warning against that brutal, erotic and overlit realm that beckons more and more persuasively to us from the margins of the technological landscape' – but few picked up on Ballard's message when the movie shifted the action to the car's spiritual home, America, from its original site on the M4.

Though speeding is dangerous, a huge proportion of drivers find speed sexy – and think of complainants as nothing more than traffic nuisances, like new road humps on a favourite backstreet route. In contrast, road safety is not sexy.

Even arch speed fan Jeremy Clarkson admits his love for fast cars could be quashed: 'If I had to argue the case for performance motoring on a Channel 5 debate programme I'd be a bit stuck. The anti lobby would only have to produce the parents of a child that had been killed by someone doing 120 on a country lane and I'd back down. They wouldn't though. They'd turn up in T-shirts with slogans and make mooing noises. And they'd have ludicrous facial topiary, through which they'd mumble something about cars killing rainforests and melting Greenland. This would be boring and, within a short time, annoying. So annoying that I'd drive home at the sort of speed a Cruise missile can only dream about.'[27]

Clarkson epitomizes our love of speed. We want to boast about it, but we hate knowing that our sleek, fast cars also kill on a daily basis. The death of Diana, Princess of Wales, puts that conundrum on to the public stage. Her Mercedes was being driven at more than 100 mph when it crashed in Paris. The driver, Henri Paul, was over the drink-drive limit. The only survivor, bodyguard Trevor Rees-Jones, was also the only one wearing his seat belt. Mercedes's S class has a reputation as one of the safest cars on the world's roads, but the fatal combination of speed, drunkenness and collision with a concrete pillar in that Seine-side underpass would have wrecked any car. Yet despite huge public interest and debate about the causes of the accident, with blame shifting from the paparazzi to the driver to secret service conspiracy theories, there was minimal coverage about why cars *can* go so fast.

It is only in Germany that cars are legally allowed to hit top speeds – and that's restricted to the autobahn. But in Germany there are very different laws relating to accidents: there, consequences do count, and as a result people can be charged for causing death by driving.

Why can most cars reach speeds twice the British legal limit of 70 mph – surely a 20 mph excess would be enough to accelerate out of trouble? Political bossyboots the European Commission is toying with the idea of bringing in a directive which will make cars less likely to injure pedestrians. This could mean all cars get raised bonnets and softer bumpers. Yet it's a move which the European Car Manufacturers' Association is resisting, claiming it will mean drivers have to pay at least £1600 in extra running costs each year for a new (that's safer) car shape.[28] Pushing the cost on to the consumer and then saying the consumer won't stand for a price hike is an industry chestnut.

But if cost is highlighted as a problem for design changes, then why doesn't the industry make cars which go more slowly? Cars could even be the whistle-blower on speed addicts. For example, a buzzer could sound when the national legal speed limit is topped. In the United Arab Emirates this already happens; sadly, drivers bypass it simply by sticking tape over the speaker. But with some design tinkering the stereo could switch off, the engine could cut out, a light could come on, the car could even tell the police . . . Outwitting your car's decision to obey the speed laws might well become a major misery for drivers in the new millennium.

It won't happen to me

During the Falklands War a bad-tempered debate in the House of Lords was brought to a halt by Lord Carrington's loyal one-liner to a peer who asked what would happen if Mrs Thatcher were run over by a bus. Lord Carrington halted that argument by snapping: 'It wouldn't dare.'[29]

Carrington had struck the mood of the times; not long after-wards, Harold Macmillan revealed that he had nicknamed his car 'Mrs Thatcher' because: 'It makes a noise if you don't fasten your seat belt, and a light starts flashing if you don't close the door. It's a very bossy car.'[30] New technology may have given us clever cars, but their programmers appear timid about what they'll boss us around on.

Some nationalities seem especially prone to spine-chilling driving – though not always getting away with it. According to P. J. O'Rourke, the residents of Beirut, Lebanon's capital city, are top of the danger league. In his book *Holidays in Hell* O'Rourke claims: 'Those who think the war is dangerous have not seen the traffic in Beirut. It's a city of a million people with three stop lights and these aren't working.'[31] Clearly, whatever the driving conditions, some people will always drive fast (the bloody fools and the show-offs). But as punk group the Buzzcocks put it in their 1978 classic 'Fast Cars': 'Sooner or later, you're gonna listen to Ralph Nader . . . Fast cars are so dangerous.' Even then it was a welcome antidote to Deep Purple's 'Highway Star' and other macho songs of car praise.

Ralph Nader's research into the dangers of driving and the self-serving, apathetic interests of the US auto industry turned him into America's leading consumer advocate. Such revela-tions, spelt out back in 1965 in *Unsafe at Any Speed*, rocked the auto industry and shocked the nation. By the expanded edition, produced in 1972, twenty-eight million defective vehicles had been recalled – but even so another 330,000 Americans had died on the highways, many of them due to known vehicle defects, including unsafe interior design and inadequate tyres.

Nader's book follows the resistance of the industry to even the most basic safety improvements. This led to auto industry chiefs being grilled by a range of senators, even though the industry was backed up by the Department of Commerce, which was well aware of the role the auto industry played in boosting gross national product. 'One business in every six is classified as automotive; one worker out of every seven is employed directly or indirectly in connection with producing, supplying, servicing, financing or transporting the automobile . . . disturb or restrict the automobile makers and you jeopardize the entire economy.'[32] Some people had spoken out against this collusion – for example, Nader quotes Senator John F. Kennedy in 1960 describing traffic accidents as: 'one of the greatest, perhaps the greatest of the nation's public health problems'.[33] This wasn't his only criticism. During the late fifties and early sixties, the Kennedy clan were outspoken critics of the auto industry – providing new meat for conspiracy theorists about just who put an end to JFK in Dallas.

Lord Beaumont of Whitley, one-time Anglican priest and now sitting on the Liberal Democrat benches in the House of Lords, is very cynical about the way the success of the economy has been gauged for so many years. In his recent book *The End of the Yellowbrick Road* he points out: 'If you want to raise gross national product (and all unthinking politicians do), here is a simple method. Get into your car and drive up the motorway causing as many accidents as you can. The boost that that will give to the automobile manufacturing, repair and insurance industries and the use of hospitals and mortuaries will be both significant and valued as such. This is in spite of the fact that authorities in this country have worked out the financial cost of a traffic incident resulting in an injury other than death as £40,000.'[34] As Beaumont shows graphically, the concept of GNP is flawed because costs borne by the environment or society (such as air pollution and loss of biodiversity) cannot be calculated – and so they are not deducted. As a result, insurance claims and a rush of work for undertakers actually boosts GNP.

Grim as this sounds, the hard-nosed economic boffins have put a price of £848,000 for a life lost on the road. In Islington, road-safety officers use a slightly lower estimate, £805,090, which means that, during 1994, 1167 people injured in traffic accidents in the borough of sun-dried tomatoes and ciabatta cost the community £17.5 million.[35] According to Andrew Evans at the Centre for Transport Studies at University College, London, 'The notion of a statistical life originated in road accidents. In the UK, the valuations we put on a life are based on the "willingness to pay" principle. In other words, how much would we be prepared to pay to reduce the risk of dying in an accident?'[36]

As drivers we know we don't have to pay that much when we exceed the speed limit, which makes putting our foot down all the more tempting. Anthony Fear, the bloke who's been clocked by police in charge of the fastest ever speeding car, after driving his Aston Martin DB7 at 154 mph on the M5 near Exeter during June 1997, was fined a mere £750 and had his licence taken away for just eight months.[37] So how much do we really need to pay to reduce the risks of dying in a car crash? What would make us act differently on the road?

Mixed messages

Around thirty million people watched Princess Diana's Westminster Abbey funeral on British TV. A week later the government's new Kill Your Speed campaign was nearly shelved – allegedly as a 'mark of respect' to the dead princess and her family. In the end the campaign went ahead, showing home videos of children who have subsequently been killed by cars. Admittedly, that's gruesome, but so is picking up a child's broken body off the tarmac. A radio version is just as arresting. One 'ad' has a mother, whose daughter was killed at the age of ten. The little girl would be twelve now, and her mum is wondering what she'd be like – before urging drivers to keep an eye on their speedometer so they don't creep over the limit.

Yet only a fortnight after the princess's funeral the nation was geeing on a British team in its bid to shatter the world land-speed record. The supersonic car, known as Thrust SSC, was driven by Andy Green to a top speed of 714.14 mph in the Nevada desert to break the record. Both the Queen and Downing Street sent their congratulations. 'Your tremendous achievement . . . is a source of great pride for the nation,' wrote the Queen.[38] A few days later Thrust SSC also broke the 750 mph sound barrier.

The land-speed smash cost around £5 million over six years. Money like that could have run several advertising campaigns to encourage drivers to kill their speed. Each run uses a staggering 300 gallons of fuel – just to fulfil a *Boy's Own* dream. Tellingly, the driver admitted that when his parachute failed to deploy at 719 mph he didn't feel scared. 'I wasn't worried at all. To be honest . . . it was quite boring.' Our love of speed is weird. The man who's been fastest finds it boring – driving is a temporary day job for this RAF pilot – whilst journalist Victoria Sharman, writing in *F1 Racing*, trills that it's the combination of sexy men and speed which gives her such a thrill: 'I know why I watch F1, you know why I watch F1, we all know why I watch F1; and it's not because I'm trying to do my bit in the struggle for sexual equality . . . I watch F1 for the same reason men watch women's tennis . . . I watch it for the talent. Young, rich and above all, talented men driving sleek, fast F1 cars at life-threatening speeds is as sexy as it gets.'[39]

So you can scrap that order for a new-reg BMW, women like Vicky just aren't going to show interest unless you're talking genuine F1 style. You won't be surprised that she isn't a *Guardian* reader either. That newspaper reported a couple of months after her story was published that men who drive too fast have become a turn-off. Though your Porsche may still notch up cred points as the car with the most sex appeal, for the sake of dating success the top speed you should consider driving it is 70 mph – and that's only on the motorway. To speed in the very unsexy Lada, or three-wheeled Robin Reliant, would be the equivalent of sending yourself to a monastery.[40] Indeed, former *Top Gear* presenter Beki Adam did just that. The turning point came when she asked, on camera, about the Chevrolet Corvette's environmental credentials and the owner gave her a blank look before saying, 'Well, it's a strange thing to ask about a sports car.' She left the show, and a few years later took life vows at a Tibetan Buddhist monastery in Scotland.[41]

Die fast, live young

'Cars have no respect for who's behind the wheel,' muttered the Rochester newsagent to his shocked customers as they re-read their Sunday papers' headlines announcing the deaths of Princess Diana and Dodi Al Fayed. He was right, but there have been many high-profile victims of the car, from the jet set –

Dodi Al Fayed's half-sister, Jemina Yassin, has seen cars kill Dodi, her father and her grandmother [42] – to royals like Princess Grace of Monaco.

The car has got film stars like James Dean, who crashed his Porsche Spyder, and Jayne Mansfield, who was decapitated in a road accident. Pop stars have a terrible track record in cars: there's Marc Bolan, who died when the Mini his girlfriend, soul singer Gloria Jones, was driving crashed into a tree on Barnes Common. Another T-Rex band member, Steve Currie, was killed fourteen years later when his car veered off the road on the drive back to his Portuguese villa. There's Eddie Cochran, whose taxi crashed late at night into a roadside lamppost on the A4, near Chippenham, throwing Cochran head-first through the windscreen. He died in hospital whilst his rock pal Gene Vincent was left with a permanent limp. There's F1 racing driver Ayrton Senna, philosopher Albert Camus and dancer Isadora Duncan, who died when her scarf became tangled in the wheel of the car in which she was travelling.

No wonder dictators have so often used the car as a weapon to remove their enemies. There is an unpleasant story of how a Malawian minister's wife was told of a fatal 'accident' even before her husband's vehicle was crashed into.[43]

Road kills

At the other end of the scale, the victims who never hit the headlines are the feathered and the four-legged. In America the Road Kill Café's concept, 'You kill it, we cook it', may be tongue-in-cheek, but for many people road kills are the only time they notice wildlife.[44] World-wide, most people tend to be blasé about running over animals. As nobody knows exactly how many animals are in the world (vets guess the total number of domestic animals from the amount of pet food sold) it's little surprise that we don't know how many get hit on UK roads.

However, drivers who hit a dog are meant to report the incident to police. But those drivers who have bothered to stop, and can see that the dog is wearing a collar, are more likely to tell its owner than the police. Problems start when the owner can't be traced: the person who's called out a vet, who might just be a kind-hearted passer-by or a policeman, is responsible for the bill. And bills can mount up; for example, a large dog with a broken front leg might need £400–£500 of treatment, including specialist orthopaedic surgery.

Currently police, vets and animal charities in Manchester are working out a system which will ensure that the welfare of the animal is met at the same time as the vet's bills. Until recently the Manchester Dogs' Home was receiving thirty hit dogs a month but staff member Brian Maltby now suggests: 'If you can't find the owner you need to notify the police. Otherwise, not only will you face picking up the bill if you take the animal to the vet, you could also be sued if you injure its spine on the way there.' But the news isn't all grim for our four-legged friends. 'Lots of dogs are knocked down, but they tend to roll, so out of thirty only three or four have extensive injuries,' says Maltby. 'The rest are bruised or shocked, or may have a broken leg. But even if they recover quickly they may still have done enormous damage to a car.'

'Stray dogs are a worse problem in the cities,' says Steve Gillian, president of Lancashire Veterinary Association, who is helping to devise a pet road traffic accident system for the Manchester area, 'but then, as far as the law is concerned, cats don't exist.' Much wildlife is invisible too.

Squashed hedgehogs only secured a press when a researcher claimed that a new breed of fleet-footed animals was developing (around the time that *Not the Nine O'Clock News* began to promote hedgehog-flavour crisps). The theory was nonsense: hedgehogs which run (unless they actually run *away* from a car) are more likely to be hit than if they roll up into a defensive ball. 'I think people notice dead hedgehogs more than other animals,' says conservationist Hugh Warwick, 'because their spines flatten and the body stays visible for a longer time than, say, a rabbit. Most of a rabbit gets nibbled away fast by other animals and birds. Also hedgehogs seem to use roads: the tarmac surface is smooth, so it doesn't tickle their tummy, and they can feed along the roadside on their favourite slugs, caterpillars and beetles.'

Hedgehogs aren't the only animals that are attracted to roads. Kangaroos have their own 'roads' and problems start when their roads cross ours – which is why Australian roads have kangaroo warning signs. But these don't stop twenty thousand kangaroo–car collisions every year. Indeed, the problem has become so bad that car makers kit many models out with bumper 'roo bars', and have developed a dummy roo, known as Roboroo, for crash-test research. Damage isn't such a problem for some of the three hundred thousand registered road-train drivers, as lorry drivers are known: some even make a sport out of hitting kangaroos. And on a typical coach journey the driver will come on to the loudspeaker after each thud in the night with hilarious lines like: 'I told you we Ozzies taught kangaroos how to fly.' One trucker, Bob Eveston, points out: 'If you hit a kangaroo nothing really happens. You get a big bump at the front, but that's the last you see of the roo. The lorry's got forty-two wheels, so if you look back there's just a bit of squashed stuff on the road.'[45]

Problem animal for drivers in Namibia is the kudu, a large antelope. Throughout that hot, dusty country drivers debate the best way to avoid hitting kudu, as a direct hit could be the death of them. It will certainly write off the vehicle. A Namibian urban myth tells of the doctor who claimed you should drive faster than the speedy kudu. For ten years he'd negotiated Namibian roads at night with success, proving the foot on the accelerator worked. Until the night when he hit a kudu. The kudu was split into four. But the doctor's body was so shattered that he had to be buried with the car.

Drivers in Sweden, Finland and Canada have similar fatal collisions with elk and moose. In Sweden there are around sixty serious car accidents involving moose each year – a moose collision even killed one of Saab's former managing directors. Recent experiments have shown that one way to stop large deer colliding with cars at night has been to fit cats' eyes along the roadside at a height which might suggest 'wolves' eyes' to elk and moose. Unfortunately, it seems that elk now prefer to avoid the 'wolves' by crossing the roads in the daytime. Nothing has yet been found to slow down Arctic Circle drivers, so when Mercedes's small car, the A class, failed the 'moose test' by tipping on to two wheels at a swerve speed of 38 mph, the company felt it had to shut its German factory for twelve weeks to redesign the car's flawed suspension – at a cost of £100 million.[46]

Bad manners

Killing an animal may seem trivial to some people, but even those that slow down for bunnies fall foul of road rage occasionally. Well-publicized incidents include the time TV star Muriel Gray, a former presenter of Channel 4's driving programme *Ride On*, allegedly chased a truck driver who had hit her car, and then punched him on the nose,[47] or Eddie Large who reportedly smashed two windows on his neighbour's Range-Rover with a golf club.[48] In theory we can all sympathize with driving stress, but it's not always so funny. Car wars and regular shooting incidents in car-dominated Los Angeles are blamed on congestion. It happens here too: a well-paid stockbroker, Frances Cernushi, deliberately knocked a medical student off his bike because he had accidentally scraped the side of her car, whilst twenty-one-year-old Stephen Cameron was stabbed to death on the M25, in front of his girlfriend, after a row with another driver.

Over the past two years two million people have been victims of outright aggression, ranging from flashing lights, 'wanker' signs and tailgating to physical assault. Nearly one and a half million have been forced to pull over or off the road, whilst 130,000 have been attacked by other drivers. Even more admit to feelings of road rage.[49] Pedestrians also have to cope with drivers shouting at them to 'get off the bloody road'. Yet few of us behave so aggressively – passing in shop doorways or crowded supermarket aisles – when we're on our own two feet.

Road rage happens when we allow ourselves to turn into monsters behind the steering wheel. That's why we give it a special name, so we can justify our own out-of-character, and out-of-order, behaviour. This is why Tracey Andrews, who was later convicted of the offence, was able to dodge charges for some months after her boyfriend was stabbed to death on an isolated country road, claiming it was an unprovoked road rage attack by a man with staring eyes.

But those staring eyes are what we'd see if we looked into our own driving mirror as we duck and dive around the lanes, hoot furiously when the person in front doesn't take off from the lights fast enough, or steal a parking space. It isn't enough that driving a car is potentially lethal; these days the act of driving appears to make some people literally murderous. Unfortunately drivers don't blame themselves for allowing their bad temper to develop; they claim that other people's bad driving habits, such as cutting in sharply after overtaking, driving too close behind or giving incorrect signals, make them

---

Olympic dreams smashed

Alex Webster's life should have been dominated by racing-bike trophies. But this top-class international racer's chance to compete for Britain in the Olympics was wrecked when a drunk driver knocked him off his bike. For three weeks Webster was unconscious. He pulled through, but his smashed legs meant he would never be an Olympic contender again. 'I got compensated,' says Webster bitterly, 'but nothing can ever compensate for missing out on the Olympics.'

I probably wouldn't have found out about Webster's Olympic loss if I hadn't been knocked off one of his mountain bikes, after trying out the excellent cycle lanes of Leicester, by a VW Polo driver opening her door into me – just two streets away from his cycle shop. I was OK, but the ripped seat of his Univega 506 triggered a few of his broken dreams. But although Webster is still reluctant to talk about the accident it didn't put him off bikes. 'It's the quickest way to get around,' he says, and to help others prove it he now runs one of the country's few bike parks, offering secure parking, lockers and showers for cyclists.

The Bike Park, Town Hall Square, Leicester LE1 9BG. (0116 299 1234).

see a justifiable shade of red.[50] It's not uncommon for people to take their work problems or sexual frustrations out on the road, using speeding and aggressive overtaking as therapy.[51]

The catch is that although most motorists think driving standards are generally bad, they think that they personally are good, even very good, drivers. Only 1 per cent admit to being bad. This national myopia means that bad driving and the risk of fatal collisions will continue to plague our roads. The only way out is for every person to have a long hard look at his or her own driving habits, plus the courage to revive or improve driving skills. As chairman of the Lex Report on Motoring Sir Trevor Chinn points out: 'The commonest cause of accidents is still driver error with bad driving habits cited as the main cause of road rage.' There is a glimmer of hope for the ladies behind the wheel, added Sir Trevor: 'Perhaps more male drivers should learn from their female counterparts, who have fewer accidents and a more responsible driving attitude on our roads.'

The power of speed

Sheer temptation is one of the biggest drawbacks in the battle for safer roads. With a smidgin of pressure on the right sole, your tin box can take on the best. For many it's irresistible. As a result some driver-safety measures, such as seat belts and airbags, have actually *increased* the likelihood of fatal collisions.

'Surviving an accident ought to improve your driving,' says risk specialist John Adams, 'but it doesn't. We all drive with our own risk thermostat, ranging from the Hell's Angel to the little old lady. Everyone drives with some propensity to take risk, so by definition there will always be accidents. For example, what seems to happen when you fit a car with better brakes is that the driver doesn't enjoy better safety because they drive faster. Safety features are seen as performance boosters. When seat belts came in there was an increase in the death of pedestrians and cyclists. So, if you turned that argument on its head, and got motorists to drive without seat belts, but with a sharp spike coming out of the steering column, safety might improve. Yes, you might see an increase in driver deaths, but other road users, like pedestrians and cyclists, would be safer.'

Adams has some other surprising solutions on the safety front. 'If it was illegal to drive with insurance I think there'd be far fewer accidents. Especially if everyone was personally liable for every accident they caused.' He has semi-tested this theory on the rare times he has borrowed a friend's car, both in the US and the UK, and knowingly driven it uninsured. 'I drove in a state of terror, aware that if there was an accident it would cost me hugely,' he admits.

Learning curve

If school standards may be said to be slipping, driving skills ought to be improving, since a forty-minute written exam became part of the driving test in January 1996. Now six out of ten people pass; it used to be nine. But when the magazine *Auto Express* sent one of its journalists to tough out the *German* test, he was humiliated to fail. In Germany L-drivers can only drive if they are supervised by a qualified instructor, and have to have a minimum of three hours' motorway driving experience, plus two hours of night driving and five hours on country roads, before they can take the test. The test may be more demanding, but better instruction means the national average pass rate in Germany is 75 per cent – considerably higher than Britain's 60 per cent mark.[52] Of course many Germans do fail their test first time round. 'It is quite hard,' says Barbara von Krudener, 'and most people fail it. Mind you, once they do pass people are obsessed by speed. Because you can go so fast on the autobahn, drivers want to go fast elsewhere too.'

'You don't have to be perfect,' the examiner told *Auto Express*'s man. 'You can make little mistakes, but not too often. But if you make a big mistake, your chance has gone.' During the course of the test he messed up at a road junction, broke a speed limit and violated a German right-of-way rule five times. Still, however many mistakes he made, few drivers could outdo Maureen Rees's record.

Maureen Rees became an unlikely TV star thanks to BBC's *Driving School*. She's not glamorous, knew nothing about cars and when behind the wheel was cantankerous to her

---

Drive better after a body overhaul [53]

- First think: Is there any other way to get where I'm going?
- Get your eyes tested – the distance in the driving test for reading a numberplate is sixty-seven feet.
- Don't drink and drive.
- Don't use drugs.
- Avoid using your mobile phone.
- Get familiar with your car, especially a new model.
- Take rests if you are tired or driving long distances.
- Keep to the speed limit.
- Concentrate at all times. Remember that in the UK six thousand accidents happen every day at speeds of less than 20 mph.
- Wear a seat belt but imagine you are not – that way you won't take fatal risks.

long-suffering husband and her driving coach, Dave, who helped her practise non-existent skills in their beaten-up Lada Riva Estate, 'Betsy'. By the end of the series twelve million people, including three driving instructors, were egging her towards success in her seventh driving test. She even starred on *This is Your Life*, securing moving testimony about her pluck and tenacity from Stirling Moss, *Top Gear*'s Quentin Willson and officers at the Cardiff police station where she cleans. Indeed, if she didn't need to get up at 3.30 a.m. and get to her job cleaning the police station, Rees might never have forced herself through repeated driving-test humiliations.

If she was driving in Honduras she could have bought her licence over the counter. It's not hard in Egypt either, as the 'test' involves driving twenty metres forward and twenty metres in reverse, whilst in the US most tests are taken in automatics – which as Maureen found is a lot easier than trying to locate the right gear as you mirror, signal and manoeuvre between exam nerves.

CHAPTER SIX

Protest and survive

Even from the hilltop church of Sacre Coeur Paris, normally one of Europe's most beautiful cities, looked decidedly ugly. It was November 1995, and a weak afternoon sun shone, so we took snaps. They don't show the Eiffel Tower, Montmartre or the Tuileries. Instead there is a dirty, mandarin-grey smudge where the thirty-mile radius of views ought to be. The people of Paris, stalled by a public transport strike, had responded with total idiocy. Instead of taking time off, they tried to drive to work. Few made it: the city was completely gridlocked and the carbon dioxide cocktail made your eyes sting.

The heady fume mix fired up one of my companions, Ceri Fielding, who clearly felt a new sympathy for the famous sixties student graffiti 'Be realistic, demand the impossible.' As the three of us tried to navigate the cobbled streets back to the sixteenth quarter his schoolboy French was dredged up in the cause of direct action. He yelled at drivers to turn their engines off (and they yelled back).

Yet even Ceri hadn't bargained on the strike causing such a problem for the audience of Paris's Green Film Festival, where his short, *To Pollok With Love*, was being shown.

To Pollok With Love is a documentary about driving a convoy of old bangers to Glasgow to be 'sacrificed' at the site of a proposed new road. It follows the classic road-movie formula: guys ('n' gals in this case) hit the road. It's the journey that counts – and on their slow cavalcade north, to the M77 extension being built against local wishes to bring fifty-three thousand vehicles daily through Strathclyde – they are clearly having fun. They drive, they stop at service stations, they have in-jokes, they fall in love, they drink black, syrupy coffee, they do a bit of protest. A poet turns up. You know they've made it to Scotland because the rain starts; and finally, behind the hypnotic sweep of windscreen wipers the bangers reach Glasgow and the Pollok Free State road protesters' camp.

To make a 'carhenge' (a cross between Stonehenge and Avesbury) the jalopies were upended in a circle of evenly spaced holes where the M77 would soon be built, and then ceremonially torched. The flaming Cortinas sent the Pollok protesters into a spontaneous frenzy of car hatred, captured both on video and by the *Independent*'s photographer. This is an anti-road road movie linking art, automobiles and environmentalism in a dramatic two fingers to the twentieth century's deadly obsession.

Though this was Ceri's first attempt at directing, and he was just using a hand-held Hi-8 video camera, the twenty-minute film secured the festival's prestigious *prix d'or*. The only glitch was that, because of the strike, Ceri didn't make it to the prize-giving. In fact he left polluted Paris on one of the last Eurostar trains out that week, still oblivious to the success of his short film.

Two years on, Paris still hasn't sorted out its traffic problems. Parisians with smarting eyes and burning throats are suffering from high levels of nitrogen dioxide, not just excess Gauloises. Indeed traffic pollution got so bad that the authorities brought in draconian car-rationing, supplemented by free public transport. By forbidding all even-numberplated cars from entering the city, they ensured that one in three vehicles stayed in the garage on 1 October. And pollution levels fell. It was a one-off measure which worked, leaving everyone in Paris a little healthier. But this 'unreasonable' halt to long-ingrained driving habits left many car drivers fuming.[1] Those who ignored the edict altogether and took to the streets – one commuter in one car – were fined.

Health alert

It's not just Paris which is getting dirtier. The notorious pea-souper fogs of 1950s London, which were meant to be brought to a quick end by the Clean Air Act (1956), have a modern successor. Again the blanket fogs are man-made, but this time the main causes are traffic pollution.[2]

The noxious cocktail caused by powering a car includes carbon dioxide, carbon monoxide, nitrogen dioxide, nitrous oxide, sulphur dioxide, soot particulates, benzene and lead from some fuel additives. It is a toxic mix which is blamed for increasing the numbers of people with asthma, heart problems and cancers.[3] The Royal Commission on Environmental Pollution claimed in 1993 that vehicle exhausts were causing 10,000 deaths each year in Britain alone. Despite this its call for strong action to slash traffic has been ignored by both the Conservative and Labour governments.

Both carbon dioxide and nitrous oxide are key greenhouse gases; and, as the Kyoto climate conference in December 1997 showed, many governments, such as the US and Australia, are reluctant to set limits on fossil-fuel emissions in case this harms their economic base. In 1971 cars produced around 12 per cent of total global CO_2 emissions from fossil fuels – and their share has been growing ever since, despite the oil price shocks of the seventies. Any improvements in emissions have been cancelled out by the increases in motor vehicles and distances travelled.[4]

Pollution is set to grow fastest in developing countries with large populations, like India and China, as their middle class turns from walking and cycling to less efficient, less healthy and dirtier ways of getting around. But the expected health toll from traffic pollution, particularly for those with breathing disorders such as asthma, may not be immediately linked to the growth in car ownership. Even in the UK, a 1996 survey by Hertfordshire County Council found that only half of those questioned realized that traffic fumes could cause environmental health problems. Yet drivers breathe in up to three times more toxic exhaust fumes than pedestrians or cyclists.[5]

There is a plus side to this: it is just possible that the return of concern about the debilitating effects of traffic may mean a renewed interest in Londoners' health. This could trigger another round of parliamentary proposals which have effects as beneficial as the Clean Air Act, which banned the burning of coal. According to Stephen Joseph at the influential lobby group Transport 2000, 'The health dimension is now changing the debate.' That's because pollution is affecting so many people – in particular children, asthmatics and people with other respiratory problems, all of which are exacerbated (if not caused) by vehicle pollution. Fan of the pedestrianized city Richard Rogers claims: 'During the winter of 1994 record levels of pollution were blamed for 155 deaths in just four days. Something like 10,000 people die each year in the UK because of emissions from vehicles . . . adding £3.9 billion per annum to the nation's medical bill.'[6]

Ringside view

The health angle gives our growing concerns about traffic a universal relevance, precisely because it affects so many people. But what has also helped feed the feeling that even if there is too much traffic there are already enough roads has been watching direct action on TV by relatively small groups of protesters. Starting with the battle to save Twyford Down, the antidote to Mrs Thatcher's rush of road-building has been opposition from committed environmental activists. Although many of the roads these groups have opposed have been built, such as the M77 and the Newbury Bypass, the roads protesters have managed to expose three myths. These are:

• Roads ease traffic congestion.
  They don't. New roads all too often encourage new traffic into an area, causing more congestion, like the M25. Even the Tories accepted this key conclusion from the SACTRA report of 1994.[7]

• Roads bring economic benefits to an area.
  Although roads may benefit some companies or driver schedules, they do not bring economic benefit to the area. They do not create new jobs. And though a new road may mean it takes ten minutes less to reach the supermarket, all roads also bring costs to the community by attracting more traffic which makes roads unsafe to cycle along or unpleasant to walk along, and may add to the likelihood of road traffic accidents and heighten noise pollution.

• Roads are beneficial to GNP.
  The problem here is definition of gross national product –

because road building and construction do not take into
account environmental costs, including loss of biodiversity
(wildlife and habitats) and the consequences of pollution,
they are seen to be a benefit even when they are not.
Ironically, funding road-building is often called 'investment',
but handouts to public transport are known as 'subsidies'.

The road protesters have also seen a halt to the road-building programme, after the 1994 review of the 1989 Roads Programme (for 330 trunk roads and motorways at a cost of around £2 billion a year).[8] That's why some say the protesters have become expert at losing the battle but winning the war – though they have also enjoyed individual successes, like getting the ancient Oxleas Wood a reprieve, and putting a final halt to the eleven-mile A36 Salisbury Bypass.

When the local MP Robert Key heard this news, he whined that the experts had succumbed to 'emotional blackmail'. The Salisbury Bypass would not have had a devastating effect on the city or Constable's famous views, he claimed: 'The new road on its modest embankment would, for the first time, allow spectacular public views of the medieval city and its landscape context.'[9] His feelings did not come as a surprise – at an *Auto Express* magazine lunch, whilst he was Minister of Roads, he announced (and one hopes he was drunk): 'I love cars. I love cars of all shapes and sizes. Cars are a good thing ... I also love roads. I have always loved roads.'[10]

Perhaps one of the greatest boosts for the protesters' morale – besides a halt to the road schemes – was the award of the prestigious Goldman Prize to Emma Must in May 1995. Awarded by the San Francisco-based Goldman Environmental Foundation and dubbed the Green Oscar, the prize gave Must £47,000 for her work 'galvanizing a movement against the national road construction programme in England'. Must, then twenty-nine, had worked as a children's librarian until she became involved in the campaign to stop the M3 extension at Twyford Down, as well as co-founding Road Alert and working with Alarm UK, which co-ordinated 250 protest groups fighting local road schemes during the mid-1990s. She spent two years organizing demonstrations and a short spell in Holloway women's prison for defying injunctions to stay away from Twyford Down.

Accepting the award, Must claimed it as 'recognition for the whole spectrum of protest, from people with beads in their hair to middle-aged ladies with pleated skirts, all of whom are opposed to the roads programme'. In the media maelstrom that followed she agreed that in the short term direct action cost taxpayers money, but pointed out that in the long term the effect would be a massive saving.[11]

These days Must works part-time at Transport 2000, the national environmental transport campaign, but she's still proud of the anti-roads protesters' successes. 'What the protesters, both the direct activists and the grassroots campaigners, did was to bring the road programme to a halt. In 1989 there were 550 schemes, now there's only 150, and they are all under review. There were three things that caused this – it was to do with public-spending cutbacks at the Treasury, the fact that the Department of Environment under Gummer began to put pressure on the Department of Transport over the roads programme and because the grassroots campaigns made it clear that the public didn't want to continue down this route. So scaling down the roads programme was a soft target for the Treasury, it could do something popular and save money.

'The grassroots focus now is anti-traffic campaigns,' adds Must. 'Very often it is people with children who are concerned about the traffic on their street and are taking action around that. Often they use imaginative stunts to lobby local councils – it's a network of people taking action for themselves which is expanding fast.'

Making changes

Roads protest is often written off as single-issue politics on the part of impassioned drop-outs, but as George Monbiot points out in his *Guardian* column, direct activists talk about a lot more than roads. 'Among those swaying tree tops at Newbury, discussions range from transport policy to the detention of immigrants, through alternative currencies, press ownership, animal welfare, structural adjustment in the Third World, land reform, air pollution, housing policy and the judiciary. Road building is top of today's list, but when the battle is over many activists will move on to something quite different.'[12]

American lawyer Ralph Nader's persistent criticism of American car and tyre manufacturers is an inspiration for many, and certainly for some of the campaigners who have found themselves whisked from suburbia to the treehouse-and-compost-toilet lifestyle of an anti-roads campaigner. Similarly, in the UK it could be said that it was the intransigence of the road lobby that helped create the roads-protest movement. One of the most damning indictments was the book written by Mick Hamer, Friends of the Earth's first transport campaigner, *Wheels Within Wheels*.[13] '[The book] showed how a small group of people with no public mandate were exerting undue influence. How they built roads no one wanted, cut rail and bus services, supported by the membership of the AA and RAC voting with their wheels.'[14] Successfully combating the protesters has been a source of pride for the motor industry. In its most recent annual report the British Roads Federation reprints a telling comment from business magazine *Management Today*: 'The BRF has only nine staff, but the "roads lobby" is spoken of with awe for its ability to persuade successive governments to minimise cuts in the road building programme.'[15]

Nevertheless the BRF is an organization which managed to promote its vision with considerable success even during Brian Mahwhinney's tentative reconsideration of road-building and traffic management during the so-called 'great transport debate'. And it's one that has the law on its side. As the direct activists have found again and again during the 1990s, opposition to roads has been met with heavy-handed tactics and a reliance on Britain's legal system to restrain protesters. Faced with the Conservative government's increasing unaccountability, people decided it was time to take matters into their own hands. The first great battle was at Twyford Down.

M3 extension: Twyford Down

The campaign to stop the cutting through Twyford Down lasted more than eight years. But as Jonathon Porritt, co-founder of the Forum for the Future and former head of Friends of the Earth, points out: 'The trauma of Twyford Down galvanized thousands of people into a host of actions that might otherwise never have been taken. It was just so horrific, so visible, so palpable. Even now, there is no amount of cosmetic landscaping and tree planting that can conceal the sheer scale of the wound inflicted on the countryside. It screams out at you, and will go on screaming out to all with ears to hear and eyes to see.'[16]

It was also the first protest where appeals to the EC, the Department of Transport, public inquiries and governmental good sense were seen to fall on deaf ears. Indeed the EC had doggedly demanded a better environmental impact assessment from the government – only to drop this as a concession to John Major over the Maastricht negotiations.[17]

Once work started groups like Earth First! and the Donga Tribe (named after Hampshire's traditional word for footpaths) staged protests – despite facing serious repercussions from the police. This added an extra £3 million to the M3 extension's £26 million bill. No wonder Twyford Down can be seen as the turning point.

M11 link road

The M11 link road through east London was first proposed back in 1962, even though work didn't begin until September 1993. During that time the community had felt increasingly ignored by the authorities. More than 370 homes were to be pulled down, after compulsory purchase by the Department of Transport. The community tried the courts, they appealed to the EC and they approached the ombudsman, but the road always triumphed.

'They're turning Wanstead into a giant traffic jam and car park. It shouldn't be like that. It's a lovely area really,' said Patsy Braga, a long-term resident, who ended up not just squatting in her house but barricading herself into a concreted room in doomed Cambridge Park, in a bid to slow down the inevitable. Bravely she whistled 'Always Look on the Bright Side of Life' – a tune which has in some ways become the roads protesters' anthem – as the security guards broke down the wall into her inner sanctuary. The final stages of the struggle by that community to stop the road being built through their homes is graphically shown in an alternative news video, award-winning documentary, You've Got to Be Choking, *produced by Undercurrents, which specializes in filming direct activists' campaigns.*

The protesters, a mix of environmentalists and local people, including a lollipop lady who was sacked for demonstrating in her uniform, did manage some temporary victories. The most famous was on 11 November 1994, when the tree on George Green, which had been transformed into a treehouse, was classified by a High Court judge at the Royal Courts of Justice as a 'dwelling' thanks to an ostentatious postbox and a letter sent from Cheshire. But the victory was short-lived: the bailiffs then sought an eviction order. In the end the tree was bashed down with a large digger. The final squatted houses got the same vandalous treatment from security guards working with eight hundred police.

The road went ahead, shortening commuters' journeys to the City. But the protesters had made their mark. 'It comes down to an economic battle. If protesters are there then companies are having to think, if we want this road, then we will have to spend £2 million in security. The costs at Wanstonia were astronomical,' says protester, Steve Brown. 'As protesters were arrested the house was being pulled down brick by brick. When you looked back it was already gone, even the stairs had been knocked down.'

A34 Newbury Bypass

For the road builders this route, crossing nine miles of countryside including three sites of special scientific interest and historic battle sites, involved removing ten thousand trees – and legions of protesters. All this for a bypass which was only going to remove 13 per cent of traffic from the town and within ten years would see both the bypass and the town in a car-crawling state. In other words it was pointless, giving added poignancy to the battles for the road being shown on TV news. Local ladies the Marchioness of Worcester and Lady Barber donned anti-roads sackcloth (green wellies and Barbour jackets) to join the woolly hats and protesters from all round the country in order to demonstrate 'that it is not just dreadlocked travellers who care about the Newbury countryside'.[18]

A30 Fairmile Bypass

After seeing that treehouses could be easily removed, the Devon protesters, some of whom had started their occupation back in 1994, tried a new tactic, underground tunnels.[19] *Here emerged Fairmile's human mole, Swampy, so-named because he was always covered in mud.*

Swampy, twenty-three-year-old Daniel Hooper, the last protester dragged out of Fairmile's tunnels, had spent seven days in Big Moma, at least eighteen feet below ground. He explained that the protesters wanted construction work to cease so that an open public inquiry could be held into all aspects of the road scheme – including building, design and finance. He didn't get that, but his own, unsolicited fame made him an obligatory pin-up for the right-on teenager's bedroom, his sweet face staring out of matted dreads, offering a Green contrast to the jagged looks of rock-and-roll stars.[20]

From an outsider's perspective the battles between protesters and security guards can seem almost surreal. *Loaded* magazine sent its reporter, Martin Deeson, to the front line. After seeing a pantomime cow arrested and hearing the protesters winding up cops with jokes like 'What do you call a line of policemen standing in the woods? A copse', Deeson decided: 'The people up the trees looked like they belonged in the final scene from *The Life of Brian* (where the hill-top is covered in dozens of blokes tied to crucifixes), then one of the protesters shouted out, "Welen Wodger!" Another yelled "Weleae Woderick!" and then "Welease Wudolf the Wed Nosed Weindeer." From off in the distance in the woods a lone voice called from what sounded like miles away, "*I'm* Bwian!" The best thing about the Battle of the Bypass is that the footsoldiers – on both sides – are young enough to be part of the E generation, and they've spent long hours consuming comedy, sci-fi and drugs. Protest has never sounded so good.'[21]

That irreverent anti-establishment energy has been captured on TV and video, and has therefore been seen by massive numbers of people. The rise of camcorder news was spurred by activists fed up with a daily diet of TV drivel. They knew that just because their campaign wasn't on the box didn't mean it wasn't not happening. So they decided to make it easy for the TV producers by providing their own footage of events. As a result, over the past few years their alternative news videos have earned a place as the new radical journalism. Simon Davies of Full On Films, who has researched a series about camcorder news for Channel 4, calls it a new global revolution, but with a twist. 'Global technology enables them to watch us. Now we can watch Big Brother,' he claims. To prove it Full On Films footage has been used in court to demonstrate the rough methods bailiffs used to remove protesters from trees during the anti-M65 campaign. 'Campaigners welcome the film-makers now as it gives them protection. Security guards stop beating people up when there's a camera running,' he adds.

The anti-roads protesters find camcorders cheap, light and simple to use. Many now do the filming themselves. You can see the results on productions like Brighton-based Conscious Cinema or Oxford-based Undercurrents, which have covered the campaign to stop Solsbury Hill Bypass; shown how the ancient custom of wassailing was used to stop road-building in Coventry; and how horses joined the protesters at the Newbury

Bypass. Some protesters' films are usually among those screened at the Green Screen Film Festival, held around the UK each February.

Resistance of the art

At Reclaim the Streets' Oxford street party in 1997, Undercurrents film-makers managed to video poet Simon Stockman as he gave an impromptu performance of his 'Homicidal Cycle Path' between a row of sombre police and a queue of exasperated motorists. Stockman claims the situation itself inspired him. 'Performance poetry makes people think. The only problem is that not enough people stop to listen to it. But when they do, poetry fires off a few synapses – nerve centres – in people's brains.'

He's not the only performer to be inspired by the energy of the roads protest movement. In summer 1996, FoE decided to turn a hundred of the 38- and 73-route London buses into mobile art and poetry galleries. FoE also organized the Newbury Art Bypass, turning a mile of the motorway into a fantasy zone. Dubbed 'up-yer-backside art', the installations included a giant snail mown into the hillside, a car sliced into pieces, plaster casts of animals killed on the road, sound and light displays, miniature concrete cars positioned as zebra crossings, and monstrous Minis. The event was devised by an FoE supporter, sculptor Clare Patey, who encouraged much of the Art Bypass exhibits to be created from reused and recycled materials. Visitors were even asked to join in the creation of a two-tonne reclining concrete goddess which could be used to block the bypass route if protesters locked themselves to her 'womb'.[22]

Times they are a-changin'

In a bid to highlight policy contradictions about transport Radical Greens block roads. Others take to them. One highly successful attempt at creating road chaos is Critical Mass, which began life in San Francisco. This direct-action bike ride has clogged up London, Edinburgh, Nottingham, Oxford, Sydney and many other cities for two hours on the last Friday of the month for the past couple of years.

'Critical Mass is an extraordinary feeling. On the way to the start you are just one cyclist out there pitting your wits against the car drivers,' says one regular on the London rides. 'Ten minutes later you are in a sweat of cyclists able to take over the roundabout above Waterloo's Bullring. As the car traffic snarls up suddenly London becomes silent. There's only the noise of hundreds of jubilant cyclists ringing bells, whistling and honking. As we snake across Waterloo Bridge, down Fleet Street and towards the City there's an immense feeling of joy. Suddenly it's quiet, it's safe and the car has been banished. Everyone notices the change: you suddenly see pub drinkers spill out on to the pavements. You can hear laughter, the flick of a cigarette lighter, clocks chime . . . and you can savour the mood of buoyancy. Critical Mass is a time when London is a great place to be.'

However, many cyclists are also car drivers, causing mixed feelings. As drivers they get irritated by the jams, but as cyclists they long for more cycle lanes, better and safer cycle-parking areas and a bigger voice during transport debates. If these don't come they use the pavement. A recent survey of London's Kensington and Chelsea residents found that cyclists on pavements were an overwhelming irritation for non-cycling residents. Yet for anyone with the temerity to pedal on pavement there are heavy fines. Cycling without due care and attention is an offence liable to a maximum fine of £2500. This is a considerably larger sum than you pay if your car kills someone through your own carelessness.

On my own two feet

Pedestrians protest too. The only time a footstep has been regarded with awe was when astronaut Neil Armstrong made his giant leap for mankind walking on the moon. The rest of the time, walking – the ultimate in environmentally friendly travel – is seen as a very humble hobby, something that people who drive don't do. As a result it's taken a long time for pedestrians' needs to be noticed. For example, most traffic-light-controlled crossings prioritize traffic flow – which leaves walkers stuck on dual-carriageway islands or busy kerbsides, breathing in exhaust fumes, as they wait for the green man to light up. And in America and Australia the pipping sound which signals that it's safe to cross is enough to bring on a serious tension headache.

Pedestrians should own the pavements. Or at least they did, until growing car ownership turned them into an ideal off-road parking space (as long as the traffic wardens didn't cotton on). To try to combat this, environmental activists around the country have taken to moving illegally parked cars themselves. Car-bouncing isn't hard at all: with just ten people you can gently rock a car off the pavement and back on to the road where it belongs. And you don't have to be that young . . .

Faith Lawson, the seventy-five-year-old former chairman of the Pedestrians Association, is tiny. But being five foot tall and weighing less than seven stone didn't stop her, and a number of other senior citizens, from bouncing around eighteen cars off the pavement along a north London street in the early 1990s.

'I'm not very strong, so it was my job to keep the police happy and make sure our group didn't do something illegal. Of course it's illegal to park your car on the pavement. When we explained that bouncing motor cars on to the carriageway was helping the police they had no answer! Once we got all the cars back on the carriageway, Chetwynd Road was so narrow that traffic could only go up it in one direction – so the police ended up with a traffic problem,' she says with a rather mischievous laugh. 'Some of the residents did argue with us or threatened to sue us for damaging their cars, but no one did.'

Not only did the protest clear the pavements, it captivated the media. 'I had photographers from all the best papers pursuing me,' says Faith Lawson, laughing again. 'I suppose they found it extraordinary to find a little old lady going about with a group of people who stop roads, live in treehouses and dig tunnels. My friends were astonished to see me on the TV too – they hadn't associated me with that sort of activity either. But everyone gets their fifteen minutes of fame!'

Faith Lawson drove for forty years, so she's very familiar with people's possessive love of their cars. 'A car is a very expensive piece of property. It's not merely a means of getting from one place to another, it's an extension of the owner's home, office and personality. People are afraid their car will get damaged and that makes them extremely possessive. People who love their car have paid a lot for it, so they want to get good value from it, and they do that by using it all the time,' she says. 'They see life in the streets from behind a steering wheel: that's totally different from the person trying to walk along the pavement – so you get a terrible conflict of interest. Demonstrations, like the car bouncing, are very useful if you can get the media there, and get enough publicity to impress people, but you also need dialogue with top authority because the government is responsible for the framework by which everyone operates.'

This step into radical action by the normally conservative Pedestrians Association (it was founded back in 1929) gave it surprising clout in Whitehall. Since then considerable strides for pedestrians have been made, including the government's commitment to a National Walking Strategy, which aims to encourage people to walk more. The Pedestrians Association has also done well in touting the concept of the virtuous pedestrian. 'This is someone who walks about, doesn't produce noxious fumes or make loud noises, doesn't bump into others and doesn't kill anyone. It could be you. Everyone can get out of their car for short journeys,' insists Faith. 'Most people are able to walk to their local newsagent, but it seems that once they have a car they have the idea that you must use it all the time. That's not necessary. You can be that virtuous pedestrian: all you need are clothes suitable for the weather and comfortable shoes.'

These days the Pedestrians Association has put its car-bouncing on hold, but the show goes on. For the past few summers campaigners from Brighton to Bristol have joined in National Boing Day, despite the police viewing the pavement's guardian angels with increasing hostility.

Bouncing cars at the seaside

Outside Brighton's train station about three dozen protesters, many from the Justice? campaign office, slowly congregate. It's lunchtime on a searing August day in 1997 and everyone is dressed in shorts and shades. As more people turn up the police issue their first warning. 'If any of you attempt to interfere with a car you're liable to an arrestable offence,' says one. It turns out that 'interfere with' means touch. One of the protesters tries to talk with the police. 'Well, we're with you then,' she says. 'If the cars are illegally parked we'll point them out to you.' And with that clear the group sets off, on foot, for the pavement-parking hot spot off St James's Street near the seafront.

Atlingworth Street has the seedy feel Brighton was once so famous for, but that's not the reason people don't walk along it. They physically can't, because cars take over the narrow pavement. Watched by three grumpy policemen, who had just called for back-up in the form of a van and three more staff, the activists started ringing doorbells to track down the vehicles' owners. A sticky-beak poked his nose through a hole in a dirty net curtain and asked what was going on. We all waited. 'Cars shouldn't be parked on the pavement because people with pushchairs or who are disabled cannot get past,' said a protester politely. A young mum leaning on a pushchair, chatting to a bloke sitting on the steps, nodded her head sagely. One van was so tightly parked to the Regency railings that its driver could only get in via the passenger seat.

At Grafton Street a driver moved his car off the pavement outside a house which sported a yellowing poster declaring: MORE ROADS? MORE CARS? MORE ASTHMA.

Again and again the police told protesters they'd be arrested if cars were touched. A man with numerous nose studs was told that if he swore again he'd be arrested. The police had no intention of calling for a traffic warden; they had no intention of enforcing parking offences. 'If we did that people would ask us why we weren't fighting crime,' a policeman told me. The protesters began to get fed up with their shadows – they were even followed into the bar of the Burlington pub. 'We're here trying to help the police,' said one woman, 'but they're trying to work against us. They're awful in Brighton.'

*It is hard to believe the intransigence of our boys in blue,
unless you are alert to the double standards operating in our
car-crazed society. Protesters are written off as scruffy trouble-
makers. Yet on the same day that the environmental protesters
were trying to make streets safer the local paper's front-page
story was PARKING HITS A HOLIDAY CRISIS – PARKING PROBLEM MUST
BE SORTED.*[23] *The Chamber of Commerce was demanding an
urgent shake-up for the town's groaning park-and-ride system,
whilst the council claimed it was trying to encourage more
people to come into town by foot, bike and bus.*

*During the summer 217,000 cars come into central Brighton
every day – yet there are only thirteen thousand parking spaces.
It's a situation made worse since two town-centre car parks
closed recently. There are hour-long queues for a space at the
Russell Road NCP and gridlock throughout the rest of the town.*

*But the people the protesters persuaded to move their cars
weren't tourists – and they weren't in any way ashamed about
their anti-social behaviour. 'That's my car,' said one mena-
cingly when he was asked how he thought a blind person would
be able to use the pavement it was blocking.*

Just about all of us believe unquestioningly that it is our democratic right to own and drive a car. The traffic gets worse, other
people make the roads dangerous, but there is no way we will
make any sacrifices for the greater good of our town. This isn't
just selfish, it's a classic tragedy of the commons. And it's
because no one will make these sacrifices; because the police
also drive their cars to work and need space to park them;
because banks spend millions on direct-mail offers for a low-
rate loan for new cars; because being given a car-parking fine
still evokes sympathy from your friends and colleagues;
because in the same *Evening Argus* as the parking crisis story

came a twenty-eight-page supplement (about half the size of the newspaper) exclusively devoted to cars and car sales, that people who protest against car crimes haven't a hope of being taken seriously, yet. Worse, they are intimidated, and in some cases arrested, for their irreverent style of good citizenship.

Partying zone

There are a number of activist groups in the UK who suffer particularly badly from heavy-handed policing. But this doesn't stop them from believing in the power of DIY politics. One such group is Reclaim the Streets, which organizes parties and protests in the cities nationwide. The group's actions may seem simplistic, but its argument is complex, warning against the perils of globalization. One of its banners points out: *'Won't the streets be better without cars? Not if all that replaces them are aisles of pedestrianized consumption or shopping "villages" safely protected from the car for its own sake. The struggle for car-free space must not be separated from the struggle against global capitalism. The streets are as full of capitalism as they are of cars and the pollution of capitalism is far more insidious.'*

Reclaim the Streets has managed to team up roads protesting with great parties. Over the years they've transformed Islington's Angel traffic lights, Camden High Street and Hammersmith into the ultimate London party venues, showing the potential of a street when it's not choked up by traffic. First it's blocked off, then up go the banners and artwork, sand goes down for the kids to mess around in and the music is turned on – sometimes provided by alternative pedal-powered set-ups like the infamous Rinky Dink sound system. It is not long before the swell of Reclaim the Streets ravers, and the curious, brings Saturday traffic to a standstill. Highlights have included sofas in Bristol, sparklers and masks at Oxford and juggling in Manchester. At Shepherd's Bush the protesters managed to infuriate police by hiding road-drilling equipment under the wide skirts of stilt walkers, and then dug up part of the M41 motorway to plant a couple of trees.

Meanwhile in Oxford a group of activists is pooling funds and scouting the smarter jumble sales so they can kit themselves out with official-looking uniforms and peaked caps. The plan is to copy an idea used by the Global Riverkeepers in the US, where self-appointed 'environmental' police make swoop raids on boat owners and holidaymakers on the waterways flooded by the Tennessee Valley Authority.

At first the victims – in Oxford this means car owners who keep their engine running in a jam – think it's the law as they are handed violation notices by courteous, efficient, authoritative environmental police officers. The notices say: *'WARNING, WARNING! You are hereby cited for failure to obey the laws of nature. Your crimes include poisoning yourself by sitting in this stationary vehicle with the engine on – even if you have the windows open . . . You are hereby required to make immediate adjustments to your behaviour.'* Once read, it is clear that despite the 'officer's' deadpan looks, this is a tongue-in-cheek arrest.

The only hitch is that scams for bogus speeding fines of £130, or demands for a court appearance, got so professional that by autumn 1997 Scotland Yard issued a warning to drivers that the genuine penalty demand (leading to more than 250,000 prosecutions in 1994) went only to the fixed penalty clerk in the Marylebone office and nowhere else.[24] Speeding-fine rackets like this could see drivers ignoring demands for legit speeding fines, but they might also mean that activists' carefully worded environmental violation notices are treated with more seriousness by the boys in blue than anticipated. A similar campaign organized by the Women's Environmental Network to tie in with Local Transport Day in March 1996 was treated calmly by police. That day women wearing BORN TO BIKE badges ticketed parked cars with leaflets highlighting the deadly effects cars have on people's health and the environment, and left ideas about positive alternatives.

You're so square

Despite Trafalgar Square suffering a twenty-four-hour-a-day, 365-day-a-year buzz of traffic, it is jam-packed with weekend rallies. In September 1997 Friends of the Earth and the Green Party held the Fuming Mad Rally there. The FoE supporters had the usual accoutrements, banners announcing groups' home towns – Leeds, Leicester, Peterborough; the Woodcraft Folk brought a giant bulbous 'world' costume clad in a gasmask. There were chants of 'Reduce traffic'; placards damning the M25 widening scheme or the Birmingham Northern Relief Road; and two cyclists with swiftly whipped-up A4 posters demanding to know if Jeremy Clarkson was a closet cyclist.

Here movers and shakers signed up to demand a new, integrated transport policy, but some of the speakers used humour as a weapon. Keynote speaker was Ben Elton, who must be the first person to have stood up and announced to the anti-roads raggle-taggle, clad in their patchwork trousers and holey woolly pullies, 'I like my car.'

Ben Elton wants us to learn highway etiquette; get quizzed on traffic-jam-ennui avoidance in our driving tests; and to stop swooning over car ads featuring smug beautiful people. 'No wonder they're smug, there's never any other cars on the roads they drive on,' quipped Elton. 'I don't care what make of car they're driving, just tell me where that road is.'

John Adams claimed the arguments against cars and roads were won over twenty-five years ago. But, from the anti-roads protesters' perspective, winning the grey-matter battle hasn't made much difference yet. That's why the protests go on.

For example, to tie in with the Climate Change conference at Kyoto in early December 1997, Reclaim the Streets squatted a disused Texaco petrol station on London's City Road, just yards from one of Texaco's flagship forecourts where pizza, dough-nuts and gift-wrapped flowers are sold alongside petrol. Within three days Reclaim the Streets had hundreds of cycle visitors checking out the impromptu Car-Free Commuter Café, after the monthly Critical Mass rally. By the Sunday the garage's altered sign – not TEXACO but TOXICO – had been photographed for the national papers and seen by millions.[25] To attract drivers a sign advertised 'free petrol' beside a twenty-foot windmill made from skip finds. A banner declaring DROUGHTS. FLOODS. FAMINE. POLLUTION. CORPORATE HELL had been hung over the abandoned forecourt canopy, and to cheer up the sober message activists had decorated it with ropes of hand-made sunflowers and 'liberated' traffic cones.

Texaco isn't the only oil company to be handed out punishing treatment. After Ken Saro-Wiwa, who had protested about Shell's despoliation of his Ogoni homeland, was hanged by the Nigerian government, protesters in London started to call the company 'Shell on earth'. Another well-used corruption is 'Shell: spoiling the planet since 1882'. And BP is referred to as 'Bloody Petroleum' by some protesters.

Steve Brown, veteran of the M11 action, was hoping the squatted Texaco station – a wind-powered, petrol-free, living, creative space – would be an inspiration for passers-by to reconsider the way they use their own cars. 'The way we live isn't right. Society as a whole has created something that most of us don't actually like, when we could have something a lot better. When you get in a car you are getting into a bubble and creating your own insular environment. This shuts you and any sense of community out. So if it gets dark, people do get frightened of being mugged because there aren't other people on the streets. And if they do walk they go past blanking you.'

Although many activists are ferociously anti-cars (in America there is even a magazine, *Auto-Free Times*, that debates only half seriously whether car drivers should be allowed to read it) Brown has an estate car. 'I call myself a car fascist. My Vauxhall Cavalier is for carrying things which I cannot carry, like the wood for that windmill,' he says, pointing at the freshly painted construction; 'it's not for giving people lifts. Without it this squat wouldn't have happened, we just wouldn't have had time to carry everything down here.'

Yet he also thinks that 'Everyone should have access to cars, but they need to be used sensibly. A lot of stuff can be carried, you don't need a car to shift it. It would be a lot better than going to the gym for exercise.'

See you in court

Rage against the machine has a long history, best-known exponents being the Luddites, the workers opposed to the rapid mechanization of the Industrial Revolution. The 1990s has brought the New Luddites.

'The Luddites invented direct action,' says Ned Ludd, 'because direct action is always against industrial forces.' Ned is not this twenty-six-year-old's real name, but Ned and Eliza

Ludd's stunts during 1996 Science Week certainly caught the attention of the national press.

'The Luddites put food on trial first, debating what price a loaf of bread should be; you could call it early supermarket action,' explains Ned. 'Later they put machines on trial. It was all democratic: they were ordinary people in extraordinary times. It made me wonder how the Green movement has ignored this huge tradition of resistance to industrialism, and one based on democratic principles, for so long.'

The first action of the New Luddites, which was set up by Ned and Eliza, was to put the car on trial. The venue was just outside York's lawcourts, in the shadow of historic Clifford's Tower where fourteen Luddites had been hanged.

At noon on a grey, March day the verdict was delivered by Sophie, the red-robed, dreadlocked 'judge', to a hundred-strong crowd that had overspilt into the English Heritage car park from the grassy knoll on which they'd been corralled by the police. When the judge found the 'car guilty of being against the common good as a means of mass transport' a pale blue Polo (circa 1978) was ritually smashed up with a giant, inflatable hammer. MAD CAR DISEASE banners were unfurled and champagne popped.

The New Luddites had invited the RAC and the British Society of Motor Manufacturers and Traders to speak for the defendants, but their non-appearance didn't mean it was a total kangaroo court. There was evidence from the 'father of the runaround', Henry Ford, and a convincing motor-industry line – but their words were weighed up against a shop owner, a local resident, a cyclist and even a bewinged angel representing all road traffic accident victims.

The event spawned a series of car trials round the country, including Birmingham and Lancaster, that summer. North

Lancashire FoE members decided against a show-trial. Instead they created a twenty-minute piece of street theatre. Once the detail was sorted out startled shoppers in Lancaster's Market Square put down their bags to watch a demonic judge call on witnesses to speak in favour of the car. Out came Henry Ford (again), plus a hammed-up local tycoon and Kevin the boy racer. Prosecution witnesses included the world's greatest cyclist Eddie Merckx (who could have inspired the joke about famous Belgians when he was awarded the title Belgian Sportsman of the Year, every year, from 1969 to 1974); a rabbit complaining that her habitat was being destroyed; and a penguin worried that global warming would be the end of life as he knew it.

With such colourful characters it was easy for the audience to sympathize when the jury found the car guilty of being a nuisance and a major cause of pollution. But the traffic-stopping show ended in near-riot when the judge then overruled the jury's decision.

'We almost took the opposite angle to what we thought,' said Mags Adams, who helped organize the action, 'so people could hear the arguments for and against the car. And we decided to make it humorous, to involve the public more.' The main dilemma was whether to use a real car in Lancaster's main pedestrian area. In the end they decided on a panto car. 'It was funny-looking, with bangers at the back which backfired very well,' added Adams. The group's first performance went down so well that they took the show on tour.

Going solo

There are many ways to change the world. Direct action doesn't suit everyone but, because the protesters' best ideas are invariably simple, they have the potential to be copied in any area – especially those over which pedestrians have some rights, for example doing a conga on a zebra crossing, or organizing a gang of mums to cross and recross at a gridlocked pedestrian-controlled light, armed with toddlers, prams and buggies. In Germany some witty cartoons were handed out showing that a granny in Kassel had to move at 9.3 kmph – considerably faster than in Hamburg (2.3 kmph) – in order to get across the pedestrian crossing.[26] Ingenious, cheap and fun – albeit irritating for drivers – ways of highlighting transport problems often also make excellent photo opportunities for the local newspaper.

CHAPTER SEVEN

Advertising gridlock

Behind the billowing incident tape outside Leicester Square's Prince Charles Cinema, tourists are beginning to gather around two cars left with their engines running, hoping to spot celebs. They are to be disappointed: the hype is just for the launch of Nissan's new car, with an expensive spoof of the seventies TV detective show *The Sweeney*. Anyone dressed in seventies gear – kipper ties, flares, even cheesecloth – and carrying a copy of London's listings magazine, *Time Out*, was nodded in to join the screening by bouncers more used to standing behind red plaited ropes. The audience consisted of journalists, fifty Regan and Carter lookalikes and the ad men. This was a première, but for a car, the Almera.[1] The idea wasn't even that original. Nissan had run an earlier parody ad for the 'all-action Almera' based on another seventies TV show, *The Professionals* – but the company and agency clearly liked the formula, and even as this was being shown another spoof ad was rumoured to be in production.

The spoof ad, produced by TBWA, only lasted minutes but it took a hundred-strong crew five days and a rumoured £600,000 to film it. The agency got it just right, using director Peter Richardson (from *Comic Strip Presents* and *Carry On Columbus*) with backdrops such as the Aldwych and London

Bridge to recall the series which turned the 'dodgy' into an art form as detectives Regan and Carter nicked villains before, during and after plastic cups of coffee and frenetic car chases around the back streets of London. It was also very funny – perfectly catching the nostalgia for all things seventies and setting off a national catchphrase, 'Shut it,' as first uttered by a grumpy Regan.

The only catch was that by copying *The Sweeney*'s style of unsafe driving, including wheel spins, fast chases and swerving through markets, Nissan received a reprimand from the ITC, which monitors ads shown on TV.

'TV ads are very powerful because they are so focused,' says Andy Wilson from ITC, which regulates all commercial stations in the UK except Eurosport. 'Adverts are meant to follow a code as much in spirit as by the letter. But the panel decided that the *Sweeney* parody of the old 1970s series, which was itself almost self-parodying, would be unlikely to influence drivers.' The ITC had a tougher line on other productions, including Ford's witty ageing of a man from 0–60 in 9.6 seconds to advertise the new Fiesta, which fell foul of the ruling that says speed may not be stressed.

'The ITC only got a handful of letters of complaint', says Nick Waters, director of the Network, part of Ogilvy & Mather advertising agency, 'for that Fiesta ad, and that was about a month after it had been running. The ITC is usually about right, but that decision was ridiculous, indicating that the British public didn't have the intellect to work out an analogy. The public can be fairly stupid, but you'd have to be pretty odd to think that seeing a face morph from baby to a sixty-year-old man would make you drive too fast.'

Waters is convinced that ads shouldn't have an effect on the way people drive; indeed, he claims that if they do then the concept-people are getting the wrong message across. They're meant to be promoting a brand, not the Brand's Hatch School of Motoring.

Clearly the ad makers thought that the *Sweeney* remake would influence people enough to buy the car, even if they also argued it wouldn't encourage them to drive badly. Indeed there's been a spate of witty remakes by the advertising industry recently. For example, Steve McQueen, who died in 1980, was 'borrowed' to star in a £20 million advertising campaign for Ford's Puma. As one advertising director put it: 'Ford has launched a new car with a dead star.'[2] What would McQueen, who was notoriously tight-fisted – but loved driving – have thought of that then? His son Chad reckons: 'It's a way to expose a younger generation to my dad, so maybe they'll explore his work.' It was also a way for Chad and his sister Terri to earn £200,000 for their dad's posthumous part. Nice work if you can get it.

The iconic comeback was such a successful ad that it came top of a poll of best ads in the industry's magazine, *Campaign*. It also led to the launch of a range of McQueen memorabilia

---

Who spends what?

Advertising expenditure 1995–6
(figures supplied by ACNielsen.MEAL)

British Airways	£18 million
Eurostar	£9 million
Friends of the Earth	£83,000
Rover Group	£42.9 million
Stagecoach Rail	£18,000

including re-releases of *Bullitt* on video and Lalo Schifrin's adrenalin-rush soundtrack on CD.

Advertising is a risky business. Good ads may pump up sales: advertising genius David Ogilvy, who has been dubbed the 'pope of modern advertising' managed to up Mercedes sales in the US from ten thousand a year to forty thousand once his Madison Avenue-based company took over the account. But in his classic look at the industry, *Ogilvy on Advertising*, he warns that some ads can also reduce sales. For example, George Hay Brown, one-time head of marketing research at Ford, inserted ads in every other copy of *Reader's Digest*, only to discover: 'At the end of the year, the people who had not been exposed to the advertising had bought more Fords than those who had.'[3]

Ad excesses

No one knows exactly how many ads are produced, although the Advertising Standards Authority estimates there are around thirty million each year in the UK. However, the trade's own body, the Advertising Association, has no record and even the authoritative ACNielsen.MEAL, which tracks advertising-spend data, cannot monitor the numbers on a product-by-product basis. 'It would be impossible to tell how many ads are produced by car manufacturers,' a representative explained; 'that ASA figure is a guess. And even if we did say how many ads were placed it wouldn't be accurate as we can't monitor every place you find adverts.'

What *can* be tracked is the amount of money advertisers spend on ads. In 1995 just forty-six car manufacturers splashed out £500 million for 15,830 press pages and three thousand radio ads in the UK.[4] No wonder it's hard to remember them all. And it's why watchers of TV and readers of newspapers know that there seem to be many more ads for cars than for any other product.

Henry Ford caught on to the power of advertising early – in 1920 *The Times* carried a scolding ad to try to turn Ford's advantage around: 'Do you know that nearly £10 million was spent last year by our own people in these islands for foreign motor products? A colossal loss to British trade and British workers. No government can cure unemployment if this sort of thing goes on. Do you realise this? You should.'[5]

Around 12 per cent of all TV ads are advertising cars. Vauxhall Motors spent a total of £58 million on ads between January and September 1997, £23 million of which was for TV campaigns. Ford Motor Company continues to be the big spender though – for the same period its total spend was more than £72 million, of which £36 million was for TV ads.[6] Compare this with the Department of the Environment, Transport and the Regions' 1997 Christmas splash-out 'Have None for the Road'. Its modest spend was £2 million to blitz potential drink-drivers over the Christmas and New Year holidays.

By 1996 around 150 different car brands were advertised on TV but, as many car models may have more than one ad made, this can mean around 225 new car commercials a year splashed into every possible media outlet. There are exceptions: one of the most famous car ads in the world, for Rolls-Royce, was only run in two newspapers and two magazines, yet its under-lining of the car's silent power ('at 60 mph the loudest noise in this new Rolls-Royce comes from the electric clock') prompted phenomenal interest amongst Americans.[7] (Though it helped that famous past Rolls owners included aspirational figures like Rudyard Kipling, Henry Ford, Lenin, Ernest Hemingway, Woodrow Wilson and Charlie Chaplin.)

Ad spend for selected motor manufacturers

January to September 1997

(figures supplied by ACNielsen.MEAL)

Ford Motor Company	£72,274,220
Vauxhall Motors	£58,368,959
Rover Group	£44,545,069
Nissan GB	£38,152,986
Audi UK	£13,443,766
Saab GB	£9,340,473
BMW GB	£8,002,591

These days most car ads are clever, highly watchable and very expensive to make. The only catch is that, without extreme imaginative effort, they all tend to look the same, falling back time and again on sex, status and safety. Advertising guru John Meszaros, who helped make Audi's 'Vorsprung Durch Technik' an eighties catchphrase, thinks ads are at a low point. 'In the first six months of 1997 around 160 commercials were used (in the UK). I can't recall too many of them – either I did not see them at all or not often enough or they were simply very forgettable.'[8]

Maybe he's got a point. Back in 1949 a Ford brochure boasted that the new model was a 'living room on wheels' – really not much different from 1997 campaigns for VW Polo, which ask, 'Have you ever noticed how safe you feel when you're small?' in their plug for the womb with a view (and accelerator). The car is often presented as an extension of home comforts and even on the road they give the illusion of a secure environment. Authors Marsh and Collett emphasize that the home-like car is a central feature of auto culture and 'this is very clearly shown by the fact that agoraphobics (those with a fear of going outside the home) are usually quite content to go out in a car, but are terrified of travelling on public transport'.[9]

Fed up non-driver Trevor Beattie, who is also creative director of ad agency GGT, wrote in his irreverent *Guardian* column recently that 'The growing legacy of utterly identical TV commercials' made him think 'it's assumed that the average car client wouldn't recognize a good idea if he came home and found his wife in bed with one'.[10]

Back in the fifties ads fuelled the idea of fantasy vehicles. This maddened acerbic critic John Keats so much that he claimed cars were 'not marketed as reliable machines for reasonable men to use, but as illusory symbols of sex, wealth and power for daydreaming nitwits to buy'.[11] Marsh and Collett sum up that era in similar terms: 'Advertisements of the time tried to suggest that by buying a particular model one would automatically enhance one's social standing, expand one's social horizons, impress the neighbours, and acquire a new sense of adventure – in short one would become a new and better person. At its very heart therefore advertising presented automobiles as a social palliative: cars were a form of psychotherapy. Nowhere was this more evident than in a TV commercial which urged the prospective owner to "drive it like you hate it . . . it's cheaper than psychiatry".'[12]

Clearly selling-ideas revolving around sex and performance have a long history. In the seventies this blatant mix resulted in the rise of *risqué* ads: big cars and undressed chicks. Renault tried to be more sophisticated in one campaign by comparing a woman's figure with their car's design – her shimmery top mimicked the metallic finish; her sitting profile inspired the padded seat and headrests and her lipstick holder the locking system.

This type of advertising prompted retaliatory feminist graffiti. A poster for a car which proclaimed: IF IT WERE A LADY IT WOULD GET ITS BOTTOM PINCHED was added to thus: IF THIS LADY WERE A CAR SHE'D RUN YOU DOWN.

Women continue to be fed up by patronizing ads. In a survey by motor retailers Cowrie in June 1996, three out of five women claimed they were patronized by TV car ads, and three-quarters felt stereotyped. The report found that women wanted more information about the car, like how much it cost and how safe it was, rather than fancy storylines, such as the ad for Peugeot 106 which tweaked the ending of the film *Thelma and Louise*. This was the era of the Vauxhall Corsa campaign which, after using supermodels Naomi Campbell and Linda Evangelista, was dropped for being sexist. Less than half the women surveyed said that TV ads had any influence on their choice of car. Nor did they care whether their nail varnish matched the dashboard.[13]

However, Peugeot's advertising manager, Andrew Didlick, who had a £40 million budget during 1996, poured scorn on this, claiming that: 'An ad that just says, "This car has four doors, a steering wheel and a gearbox" is boring.' Clearly he thinks there is plenty of mileage left in auto sexuality.

Sexual selling isn't the only bugbear. Transport campaigner Don Matthews worked at Friends of the Earth in the eighties, and remembers being furious at Toyota's ad of a Celica Supra being fired from the barrel of a gun with the slogan 'More like a bullet than a bullet – the trigger is under your right foot.' Matthews complained to the Advertising Standards Authority, 'set up to stamp out such nonsense', as he puts it, but 'alas, the ASA seem to be hand-wringing wimps of the first order. It was obvious that the ASA was quite unable to enforce their own code.' To counter-attack, FoE campaigners plastered offending ads with a Grim Reaper and scythe. In all a total of twenty-two sites got the Grim Reaper treatment, the campaign only stopping when the police confiscated the last Grim Reaper.

Even though blatantly sexist ads may not be acceptable now, ads extolling the qualities of speed and power still are. 'Ads are allowed to blather on about performance because that's a selling factor, like the torque and horsepower,' says Nick Waters. 'The danger is that if companies said they were producing the cleanest, Greenest car it would mean environmentalists might uncover information that showed it was completely untrue. Car companies are major manufacturers – and all major manufacturers tend to produce a tremendous amount of waste. Also there's greater Green parity through legislation so environmental qualities are not a marketing angle, though they could be if a car was particularly fuel efficient. But for petrol-powered cars that's a nonsense. Really clean cars, the concept cars, are electric or powered by alternative fuels, but they aren't on sale. If they were it would kill the oil industry.'

Environmental writer John Whitelegg recognizes that this puts advertisers' efforts to market cars between a rock and a hard place. 'People believe cars offer freedom, power, sexual fantasy and reinforcement of personal esteem and ego. The fact that most of this applies to men and not women has not gone unnoticed in the advertising world . . . Sex, freedom, and power score very highly as behavioural drivers and motivators. Going by bike, walking or catching the bus are not likely to conjure up anywhere near as powerful a cocktail. It is for these reasons that inducements to leave the car at home or use an alternative mode of transport have to be equally powerful and cover as many policy angles as it is possible to design.'[14]

To date it hasn't been easy to persuade people to leave the car at home. 'Although you can't shame people out of cars with adverts you could probably get them to modify their use of cars if you can relate the message to health issues as well,' reckons the chief executive of Hill Murray advertising agency, Stephen Chipperfield. 'Advertising can create cultural change; drink driving after all was a bit of a laugh twenty years ago, but now it is socially unacceptable. But it would be hard to get away with spending less than £3 million a year over a five-year commitment – and even that would still be only a sixth of what a company like Rover spends advertising cars each year.'

To keep a check on advertising excesses in the print media there is also the industry's self-regulation body, the Advertising Standards Authority (ASA). Over the past decade it has tightened up its code, and introduced a special section on motoring in 1995. The aim was to quash the concern that agencies were producing ads with too much focus on speed and performance which could encourage bad driving by the public. But despite these efforts the ASA has recently warned that speeding is creeping back into the ads. This has led to a ban for the Volvo S70 T5 ad, which had copy boasting that: 'Overtaking is a simple undertaking' when you could reach speeds of 152 mph – 'should you find yourself on the autobahn, of course'.

'Autobahn speeds are not legal in the UK,' said the ASA's director of communications Caroline Crawford, who is a self-confessed fan of driving, 'and this ad is using weasel words, which we won't tolerate.' Other car ads banned by the ASA for making much of speed include ones for the Citroën Saxo and the Nissan Primera.

The Audi 100 saw two of its campaigns slammed by the ASA, including the 1992 images of a car taking off from a country road. The car was supposedly in a rally situation, but the hook line was 'When I tap the dashboard, take the next corner at 90 mph.' Audi's ad agency was not just playing up the car's speed – the previous year it was also willing to claim that another model was 'one of the safest cars ever tested'. However, when a suspicious ASA asked for evidence it found the claim was false, resulting in embarrassing publicity for Audi.

Yet it's the allure of speed, freedom – and empty roads – which advertisers fall back on time and again. 'Isn't it time we got real?' says comic and novelist Ben Elton. 'These images are out of date. We've got to get to grips with reality. I like my car. We all like our cars. But we've all got this problem – we all want to visit the same pubs and theatres. We're vandalizing Britain. Not for the freedom of the car ads but to sit in more traffic jams. How often have we heard it said: With freedom comes responsibility – and the greatest way to lose that freedom is to abuse it.'

'It's a good point, but to be honest the reason ads show cars on open roads is to give the ultimate driving scenario,' says Angus Ogilvy-Stuart, associate director at Universal McCann. 'If you are trying to sell a car you're not going to show drivers hot and bothered in a traffic jam. You want to show the fun of turning a tight corner or putting your foot down a bit. It makes sense, you sell things in an ideal light,' says Ogilvy-Stuart, who has worked on the Saab account. 'TV is the best medium to reach lots of people, especially if you are trying to build up people's perceptions of a car brand. For example, if over a long time a manufacturer is investing money into the image of a car brand you are building a set of credentials in people's minds, so even if they can't afford that car now, or don't want it now, when they do want to buy and have the disposable income you will have already built up the images, style and positive perceptions of that brand. This might be the look of the car, or its credentials on safety or the environment, or its reputation as a robust, strong car. The ads are a pre-sell before the dealers start selling.'

It's hard to know how taken in potential car buyers are by these dreams, though there appears to be a new tendency towards realism (albeit still with good-looking actors), begun by Ford's celebration of its twenty-one years as the 'market leader'. And a recent Vauxhall ad portrayed the new gridlocked world with considerable flair, depicting a man losing his temper because his car is stuck in a jam. Meanwhile in the same jam, a woman driving the air-conditioned Vectra sits cool and relaxed. It's a trend we're likely to see more of, given that stationary is the reality for most urban drivers.

From car-free roads to car-free ads

Researchers have found that 12 per cent of Brits actually spend more time in their car than they do with their family.[15] During the first three months of 1997 more than thirty million work hours were lost to motorway traffic jams; in total forty-six million vehicles were involved.[16] Whatever it used to be, it's no longer quicker by car. Twenty years ago Ivan Illich's classic book *Energy and Equity*[17] graphically pointed out that drivers' refusal to do their sums explained why industrial societies stayed wedded to their cars. 'The typical American devotes more than 1,500 hours a year (which is 30 hours a week, or four hours a day, including Sundays) to his car. This includes the time spent behind the wheel, both in motion and stopped, the hours of work to pay for it and to pay for gas, tires, tolls, insurance, tickets, and taxes . . . A good part of each day's work goes to pay for the travel necessary to get to work . . . It takes this American 1,500 hours to go 6,000 miles (in the course of a year). Three and a half miles take him one hour.'[18] Illich cannot resist pointing out that 'In countries that do not have a transportation industry, people travel at exactly this speed on foot, with the added advantage that they can go wherever they want and aren't restricted to asphalt roads.'[19]

Perhaps that's why car ads are changing. The best have always avoided falling back on the vroom-around-scenic-hairpin-bends. In the industry the Fiat Strada's launch ad is still considered brilliant – the only problem was that it was a rotten car. The long-running story around Nicole, Papa and their mutual passion for the Renault Clio has survived nearly six years but even it is tiring and can expect to face the axe, just like the Vauxhall Astra ad with Tom Conti and Nigel Hawthorne. Nick Waters at the Network predicts that the next generation of car ads won't feature the car. Already Ford's launch of the Ka was done without that odd, pessary-shaped vehicle, and upcoming Fiesta ads take a similar car-free approach. 'The days of the car on the open road are over,' he says. 'It was always hackneyed, clichéd nonsense.'

So it seems we're not all taken in by glamorous ads. The *Independent*'s Gavin Green, after test-driving most of the new 'people carriers', confirmed this when he plumped for a plain workhorse, a Fiat Ulysee turbodiesel. 'It looks about as interesting as a cardboard box: a modern, bland, van-like thing. But there is such a pleasing unpretentiousness about it. It handles well, rides well, seems well-made, is economical and goes about its task in a no-nonsense way. It was refreshing to drive a car that has no trumped-up advertising-led image and doesn't pretend to be aggressive/sexy/individual/superior/fiery/sporty/caring or in any way anthropomorphic. It is just a vehicle, no more or less, it carries a lot of people, and it does a good job.'[20]

Hard sell

If advertising sells cars, then surely it can be used to sell the alternatives, to entice people out of them. 'We're trying to aim at the positive by saying, "Drive less and your life will be better: you'll feel fitter and you and your children will breathe more easily". We wanted to point out the contradictions to people and explore myths about why people use their cars,' explains Lilian Goldberg, who works on Hertfordshire County Council's Travelwise initiative. 'The ad campaign was done in a slightly satirical, joky way, and pointed out that you don't need a car to buy a newspaper.' With a modest spend of around £5500 the ads were broadcast on GLR during June 1996 to tie in with Green Transport Week, Walk to School Week, Child Safety Week, National Bike Week and Don't Choke Britain Month. There were also posters depicting families on a walk with the reminder that this was how you could best enjoy fresh air. The not entirely convincing message was: 'Leave the car at home – call 01992 555999 for all the details.'

Friends of the Earth used a much more aggressive advertising campaign, at a cost of around £12,000, to highlight its Cars Cost the Earth campaign. For one week drivers stuck behind buses in London, Belfast and Manchester were challenged by a message on the back of the bus: DON'T JUST SIT THERE FUMING . . . supported by facts and figures designed to look like clouds of pollution.

'If the government announced it was to run an advertising campaign about the impacts of driving it would make it easier for them to introduce alternatives, like public transport, cycling and walking, and enable a move away from road-building,' reckons FoE's senior transport campaigner, Roger Higman. 'The key role for advertising is political change, not personal.'

But Hampshire transport planner Peter Brown is adamant that advertising is a dead end. 'Even if we were given £60,000 tomorrow we wouldn't start advertising as a way of getting people out of cars, as we've convinced ourselves that advertising only works in the short term.' The crunch point came with analysis of how the use of seat belts was sold to the public – for around twenty years, through adverts using the likes of Jimmy Savile with the 'Clunk, Click' catchphrase – until it was finally made law in 1983.

Brown didn't always think that advertising was ineffective: Hampshire's attempt to reduce people's dependency on cars, part of its Headstart initiative, was set to be launched with a £60,000 six-week TV advertising campaign on Meridian. 'It was specially commissioned, and it was good,' recalls Brown. 'It started with a kid singing (to the tune of "One Man Went to Mow"):

> "One man and his car
> Caused a jam in Hampshire,
> Ten men, nine men, eight men (and so on)
> Caused a jam in Hampshire."'

Not content with creating a hummable plug, the ad then appealed to viewers' common sense, asking them: 'Are you driving Hampshire to a standstill? Use your head, not your car.' But the ad was never run because the authority was warned that if the campaign didn't work a great deal of money would have been wasted – and some local people alienated.

'We pulled back because people feel protective about their cars; they'd have thrown at us things like "What's the council doing spending £60,000 on this when old people in homes are not being looked after properly and what's the council doing anyway letting its chief officers drive big cars?" Instead we've developed a long-term community approach in which we hope to win people's hearts and minds.'

Investigative deadline

The jury may still be out over whether ads can coax people into using their cars less, but the definitive answer may be revealed in August 1998. This claim comes from the director of the University of Westminster's Transport Studies Group, Peter Jones, who is co-ordinating a £600,000 project to investigate just this issue.

'Our project is designed to answer the question: Can you use ads to get people to get out of their cars?' said Jones, who submitted the project to the European Commission for funding, known as Inphormm (Information and Publicity Helping the Objective of Reducing Motorized Mobility), with German company Socialdata; a Spanish consultancy group; Swedish consultancy Marknads Komunikation; together with four associated partners: Hertfordshire and Hampshire County Councils, the City Authority in San Sebastián, Spain; and the Public Transport Authority of the Venice region, Italy. The twenty-month project, which saw Jones joined by a full-time researcher, will study past attempts around Europe to provide travellers with alternatives to cars, and campaigns set up in a bid to tempt locals to use cars less.

CHAPTER EIGHT

Get moving

In the late nineteenth century, William Morris felt London needed a redesign; the best way to start would be to plant an orchard of apples and apricots at Trafalgar Square. Morris's car-free vision lives on with the work of architect Richard Rogers, who wants to reroute traffic in London so that both the Embankment, stretching from Parliament to Blackfriars Bridge, and Trafalgar Square could become car-free. He doesn't stop there, with plans to free Shepherd's Bush, Brixton and the appalling Elephant & Castle from the tyranny of twenty-four-hour bump and gear-grind.[1]

Things *can* be different. Cars were banned from the centre of the Dutch city of Groningen as long ago as September 1978.[2] Now this city of 170,000 people sees 70 per cent of journeys around it made by bike. There are bike-hire shops and bike garages at the bus station, and bus links to the train station. Even though private cars are banned, getting around couldn't be easier – and that's attracted prestige companies to site their headquarters in the city, including the Dutch Post Office and the national gas utility.

In March 1992 people in Amsterdam voted in their first ever referendum to ban the thirty-five thousand cars which drove into the centre of the canal-crossed city each day. Strasbourg has banned cars from its centre. Zermatt, the Swiss village resort at the foot of the Matterhorn, forbids cars, though there are a train station, electric taxis and horse-drawn carriages. York has pedestrianized around thirty streets. But a total ban isn't always the way to civilize cities: in the Brazilian city of Curitiba, car use has been slashed by developing a fast, cheap surface metro which shifts 1,300,000 passengers every day.

Denis O'Hagan, head of the Transportation Unit at the Department of the Environment in Belfast, has helped put an integrated transport policy in place in Northern Ireland – though he claims his job has been made easier by just one authority being responsible for roads, and because Northern Ireland has a regulated system of public transport provided by a joint bus/rail operation, Translink. Even so he admits: 'There is a sense that we are going to have quite a struggle to get people out of their cars in Belfast, especially if the alternative is to get on a bus which is also involved in delays.'

Although he usually drives to his office, he has started to take the bus a couple of days a week. 'I suspect I'm the only person on the bus by choice, but whether people don't use buses because it is a stigma, or because they perceive the car as an easier, cheaper alternative isn't clear,' he says. However, the city is planning to have a special bus lane introduced during peak travel times on the already red-painted hard shoulder of the motorway before 2000, which may help encourage a change in driving habits.

In Edinburgh too the transport team have ditched their cars. 'There's been a conscious effort by senior management not to use cars and to eliminate their parking space so it can be used for a cycle park,' says John Saunders, policy manager of the

City Development Department at City of Edinburgh Council, who faces a twenty-five-minute walk to work each day. Other members of the team use the bus, cycle or take a train. 'We want Edinburgh to be a civilized city, not one physically dominated by cars and roads.'

Building utopia

Significant changes can be made by both transport managers and planners – such as car-free housing estates. The first car-free area to be developed was Hollerland, in Bremen, Germany, in 1992, and though this has been wound up a smaller scheme at Grünenstrasse has been successful. According to author John Whitelegg: 'Residents living on the estate undertake not to own a car, and only a few parking spaces are provided (these are mostly for visitors to the area). A car sharing scheme is available for the resident to use, but it is assumed that most journeys will be undertaken by public transport, walking or by bicycle. So far demand to live on the estate has been very high, as the space that would have been taken up with roads, garages and parking spaces has been used to provide green space, a kindergarten and play space for children. It is expected that pollution levels and accident rates will be lower.'[3]

There are now around thirty such housing developments in Germany and also similar set-ups in Amsterdam, Rotterdam and Vienna, but still the car-free idea is only slowly being accepted in the UK, with the lead being taken by the central London Borough of Camden.

The first private car-free development in the UK should see forty-one executive homes on sale by summer 1998 at 25 Farringdon Road. This will be followed by twenty-nine housing-association units at Stuckley Street in Covent Garden.

'The idea came from looking at the problems we've got because Camden is a central borough with so many cars. Not only have there been an increasing number of complaints about pollution but also more and more about providing parking spaces,' says Rosie Brocklehurst, from Camden's Environment Department. 'The pressure for resident parking bays is intense.'

Residents on car-free estates will be told they cannot keep a vehicle and they will not be able to purchase a parking permit. There may be teething problems, admits Brocklehurst. 'It's like trying to introduce a utopia in one small area – and because everything is imperfect it won't be utopia. We expect there will be carpers and cynics saying it's a utopian dream, but equally there will be people paying £150,000 precisely because the houses are car-free. They'll know that the area will still be polluted, but they're making a clear life statement. And then over time Camden expects to build up pedestrian areas in the borough. By 2000 hopefully there will be a strategic look at London's traffic problems with the new Central London Authority, and that may mean more controlled parking zones, Green traffic schemes and better public transport. Gradually people will find the pressure to have a car in the city becomes less. And that means over time there will be benefit for a lot of people, not just people in isolated areas.'

The only major snag Brocklehurst envisages is that the process will take considerable time: she expects marked improvement by 2050. However, for planners considering car-free estates she warns that it is vital to have full public consultation. 'Everyone must know what to expect, and know that if they keep a car there will be penalties. Where pets are banned landlords may turn a blind eye to a cat, but they wouldn't be able to do that with cars on a car-free estate because it would cause furore amongst the other tenants,' she adds.

Edinburgh's Gorgie Goods Yard Development won't be ready until 2000, but it looks set to be the biggest car-free estate in the country, with 120 housing units. Edinburgh heard about the idea of car-free estates from the Car-Free Cities Network, a pan-European group including Copenhagen, Bremen, Sintra (Portugal), Barcelona, Strasbourg, Palermo, Nottingham, Birmingham and Glasgow. 'You don't have to prove your credentials to be a member, but in a sense you are making a statement by signing up to an organization which calls itself car-free,' says John Saunders at the City of Edinburgh Council. 'Gorgie Goods, a former railway sidings, is being developed by a housing association but the council saw it as providing new housing choice. Everywhere that you live is surrounded by cars, and you have no choice in the matter, whether you have a car or not. This is an imaginative scheme which has been promoted as having a low environmental impact. There's a degree of scepticism but mostly people are very enthusiastic.'

Home zones

A similar idea, home zones (known as *woonerf* in the Netherlands), has been growing in popularity around Europe. These are streets where people have priority and cars may only travel at walking pace. Home zones are marked by road signs but typically the roads are reduced in size so that pedestrians aren't restricted to narrow pavements, making them safe places for young children to play and cutting down on noise and pollution levels. Such schemes are often boosted by attempts to green the street with raised planters and trees. Already the Netherlands has introduced more than 6500 home-zone streets. They are also popular throughout Germany, Austria and

Denmark. As for cost: a street of around five hundred metres could be transformed for around £15,000.[4] Better still, up to 80 per cent of roads in urban areas could be made safer by governments agreeing a 20 mph speed limit.

Sweet change

In York, the council has worked hard to make the streets fit for people to enjoy again. As a result, the historic city has one of the most effective transport strategies in the country. Ten years ago, York smelt different. When the wind blew from the north there was still the sweet scent of sugar beet, and on Wednesdays a distinct minty hint that After Eights were being made downwind at Rowntree's, but most people inside the city walls were more aware of choking car fumes. York still has traffic jams, especially during the early-morning rush of forty thousand cars, but now that the city has three out-of-town car parks (there is even talk of a park-and-sail scheme along the River Ouse) and more than thirty-five pedestrianized streets in the town centre, York is a better place to be.

Instead of the roar of traffic you can hear your footsteps padding along the streets. You can pick up the heady scent of Taylor's coffee roasting in Stonegate, and American aftershaves from tourists queueing outside Betty's teashop. Instead of locals, students and tourists dodging diesel and death, people dodge people. On the day I visited John Bann, head of transport planning at the City of York Council, there were even peacocks crossing the cobbled streets near the fourteen-strong transport team's office.

'To make changes, the main things you need to understand are the problems in your own location. The congestion, pollution, delays, traffic speeds, pedestrian conflict, level of accidents . . . and you need to know what might happen in twenty years' time, for example more industrial sites and more people, which will mean more traffic.' With this kind of vision, you soon realize that Bann is an organized person. His large attic office has a look of ordered chaos, but when he stops the interview to find a prized road report, point at the map of York or a news clipping, he has no hesitation about where to locate it – which makes the frivolous Mr Funny tie he sports fractionally unsettling. Bann wanted to be a planner from the day he saw a United Nations film about planning in the Third World during a school trip. His first degree was in geography, taken at Newcastle, but this was boosted with a master's in transport planning at Leeds. Once qualified, jobs were no problem – the only hitch was trying to ensure that he could cycle to the office. For the past eight years at York this has involved a riverside pedal from the commuter suburb of Fulford straight into town.

York is streets ahead of other British cities when it comes to improved environments. For starters, it has one of the largest pedestrianized areas in Europe, and has been singled out for praise by both the Conservatives and Labour.[5] During his time as Transport Minister, Steven Norris claimed that in York 'I have seen a twenty-first-century approach to handling traffic problems.'

Even so, there wasn't much funding on offer – a factor most local authorities have to face. To implement its transport changes York hoped to spend £2 million annually over ten years, with a finish date in 2006. Instead the city was promised £600,000 a year – a derisory sum when contrasted with the cost of a traffic-calming scheme being implemented in Gloucester (£5 million over five years) or the £169 million spent on less than six kilometres of motorway forming the Manchester Outer

Ring Road (linking the M62, M63 and M66) around Bann's home town. But, even if progress has to be slow, there is still a steady stream of visitors hoping to copy York's success. They've come from Holland, Belgium, Japan, Canterbury, Manchester, Winchester, Stirling and Stoke-on-Trent . . . and the list keeps growing.

'As everyone has an opinion about transport, everyone also thinks they know of a solution. It's not like education, where you don't think about it once you've left school until you have your own children; or health, which you think about only if you or someone you know gets ill. Transport affects everyone, every day: even if you're housebound, lack of transport restricts your ability to do things,' says Bann. 'The point is, most people don't get in their cars to drive – even "going for a drive" is more about appreciating the countryside. They drive to get somewhere or do something.'

Despite this drive to drive, under the local council's direction York has cut accident rates on the roads. Cyclists make up 15 per cent of all journeys, many using the thirty-five kilometres of designated cycle routes; rush-hour car usage has stabilized at 1992 levels; there is improved priority for buses, cyclists and pedestrians and minimal road-building. The knock-on effects have boosted tourism and local business. One estate agent, Hillier Parker, found that property in streets which had been pedestrianized secured higher rents.[6]

It's not all perfect though, admits Bann. 'We still have some traffic difficulties. For example, we've had gridlock in the city where people can't get out of a jam for a number of hours. If we hadn't considered the big picture that situation would have increased, and so would pollution.' It's a scenario that Bann has been watching re-enacted across the world in Michael Palin's most recent TV series, *Full Circle*.

'In York there was a backlash after we paved the city-centre area. People thought we were just doing it for the tourists. People have to have a better understanding about transport strategies so they are able to appreciate that any changes are not just to be anti-social.'

In York the council tried to involve the city residents and regular shoppers, with an architectural competition and also a panoply of surveys. 'We were quite surprised by how radical some ordinary people's views are,' says Bann. 'There's been some research in Germany which has shown that politicians are always more cautious about what changes the electorate want than the electorate is. This doesn't mean to say there isn't resistance to change though.'

In York they've used a classic formula. There are sticks (parking fines and residents' parking) and there are carrots (free stays at the park-and-ride, though you still have to pay for the bus journey into town; cycle routes; better pedestrian facilities and some subsidized bus routes). Two extra ingredients have helped: the city's outer ring road, completed back in 1988, a year before the transport strategy took off, which helps keep journeys into York limited to the essential; and from the mid-eighties onwards there has been a set of controlling councillors who wanted to pedestrianize the city.

Does this make Bann sound anti-car? It shouldn't. He drives, and points out: 'I can understand people's interest in cars. I can appreciate the craftsmanship – there are some lovely machines. And I can understand people's dependence on cars, especially people who live in villages and work in cities. Cars have given us a great deal of freedom, but people can't have unlimited use of their car. I'd hope that Jeremy Clarkson, being an intelligent chap, realizes that if ten thousand others get in their cars, you end up with a traffic jam. And as society becomes more affluent, we seem to end up with more cars. There have to be limits though – perhaps we will end up with a policy like Chinese birth control, one car per household,' he says with a slight smile. 'We can license which cars are allowed in the city, we can tax more, or we can use our cars less voluntarily, like walking to the paper shop. I can imagine people thinking, Great, I live in mid-Sussex, I can't do that, I need my car. But we could all start to use alternatives, like the park-and-ride here in York or by encouraging our kids to walk to school' – the method his own two children use. 'The aim is sustainability. If we don't change there's going to be a disaster.'

Public transport

Streetcars of desire

There is a huge range of public transport alternatives available throughout Britain. In the UK the golden age of trams was during the first twenty years of the twentieth century. At first, around 1860, they were powered by horses, along lines laid in London and Birkenhead, with most of Britain's large towns doing the same over the next thirty years. A real advance came with electric traction, first introduced in Blackpool in 1885, which spread rapidly between 1895 and 1910.

Decline started after World War I and was intensified with the introduction of all-enclosed double-decker buses and electric trolleybuses in the late 1920s. The alleged congestion trams caused to the ever-increasing number of private motorists was another significant death knell. Except for Blackpool, with its popular seafront line, all other British towns eventually lost their trams, the last to go being Glasgow, in 1962. In contrast modern-ization occurred overseas: St Petersburg and Vienna are examples of large cities still criss-crossed with street tramways, whilst taking a tram is a quintessential part of a visit to Amsterdam, Melbourne or San Francisco – not just for their rarity value, but because the routes take you where you want to go.

Now, after trams have spent years out of fashion, some British towns are tempted to turn to them again. There are already operating stretches in Manchester and Sheffield. Construction is under way at Birmingham, whilst a bill giving the go-ahead to Croydon's tramway forty-three years after it was closed was signed in July 1994.

But is the UK's tram renaissance merely nostalgia? Certainly that's the view of John Meredith, joint author of the ultimate anoraks' guides Croydon's Tramways *and* Clapham and Streatham Tramways.

'Trams are a gimmick now and don't make too much sense in the UK,' claims Meredith. 'It's not just the expense of building them – once they have been got rid of it's extremely difficult to fit them in existing towns. Building Sheffield's caused massive disruption to the city. Worse, neither Sheffield's nor Croydon's new trams actually go where people want to go. In Sheffield the Supertrams have a poor interchange at the station, endure lengthy delays at Elm Tree traffic lights, get held up by buses in West Street and are caught in road traffic congestion at Hillsborough. Worse still, the system was designed to serve some major blocks of flats which were closed between planning and opening. At Croydon one of three Tramlink routes will make use of a former British Rail train line that crosses a sparsely populated area: it's mostly marshes.'

Tramways, like those in Manchester, are cheaper to build than underground railways, such as the Newcastle Metro, and they are better for short distances. But the key to the success of any public transport is that it goes where people want to go, and goes there frequently, ideally every five minutes. And to stop delays people need to be able to pre-pay for their tickets.

The city which is always cited as having managed to get people out of their cars and on to the buses is Curitiba, despite its 1.6 million residents having some of the highest car-ownership levels in Brazil. Here a 'surface metro' has been installed, with stops every four hundred metres. To speed up the service passengers pay for their fares at ticket machines sited at the stops.

Guiding light

Surface metros and 'guided bus' services are much cheaper to build than tramways. Both are essentially just buses, so often all that's needed is a raised kerb and dedicated lanes to keep other traffic out. There are excellent guided buses in Adelaide and a much-hyped short stretch in Leeds. Oxford has hopes of setting up a guided transit express system, with vehicles switching from rail to road, by 2005. However, a cheaper method of prioritizing buses is to cover one lane of a highway in red paint and forbid all other vehicles, something already being trialled in Leicester and on the M40 link to Heathrow Airport.

Gas-powered buses

At Northampton efforts to improve public transport have seen teamwork between the council and the local bus operator, Northampton Transport, with the introduction of gas-powered buses. On a three-mile stretch known as the Northern Corridor which links the Kingsthorpe suburb with the city centre, the council has built bus shelters and raised kerbs, whilst the bus company has obtained six buses – which cost around £20,000 more than their diesel counterparts – with special low floor entrances to make them easily accessible to the disabled, the less able and the pushchair set. The service has also been increased from every fifteen minutes to every ten. 'It's a pilot scheme,' says Andy Berncastle, public transport manager, 'and we haven't done any surveys yet, but at least Northampton is catching up with other towns.'

Park-and-ride

Even if drastic changes are rare in the traffic-management world, the subtle process of curbing the car often seems to involve parking changes combined with improved public transport. The classic example is park-and-ride, first introduced in Oxford in December 1973. 'However good public transport is, if you don't restrain the car by parking measures people will choose to drive into towns,' says Alan Diver, chief assistant engineer, highways and transport, at Oxford City Council. 'That's why residents' parking has spread. If people have access to a free parking space we've found they'll use it regardless.'

Oxford City Council calculates that its park-and-ride facilities take four thousand cars off the road on weekdays and nearly five thousand on Saturdays – approximately 1.7 million people a year. 'We estimate that a third of the people parking at Thornhill park-and-ride use the Oxford–London bus services, which stops them from coming into the city. Park-and-ride sites are also used by people who drive to them and then cycle into Oxford, rather than use the buses,' adds Diver.

Park-and-ride has its critics. For starters it means people still have to rely on their cars. Secondly it dumps large numbers of cars on newly created tarmac sites, often at the edge of towns on green-belt land. The Council for the Protection of Rural

England has also pointed out that this leads to increased suburb-anization of the countryside as signs advertising the park-and-ride service creep into rural sites.

'By definition park-and-ride is on the edge of the city,' agrees Diver, 'but another problem is the conflict between personal security and too much vegetation, which is put there to make it look pretty. At times we have felt under pressure from police to remove trees and shrubs to stop miscreants hiding behind them. There is also the issue of whether by having park-and-ride on the edge of an urban area you encourage people to drive through the countryside to it. Where people have the option

My friends think I'm weird

Fittingly, the front-of-house manager at the London Transport Museum in Covent Garden swears by public transport. Stuart Hobday's friends never tire of asking when he's going to learn to drive – but Stuart's just not interested. 'I was never into cars as a kid, so there was no rush to drive. Then when I was twenty-one I was in a bad crash, which I think confirmed my suspicion of cars, and made me more resolved to cope without one.'

That's when Stuart found dating took a serious U-turn: 'Women look at you as if you've got two heads when you tell them you don't drive,' says Stuart with a grin, 'and it's definitely contributed to innumerable unsuccessful first dates!

'But as I've got older there's another reason not to bother to learn: the environment. Yes, my friends think I'm a bit weird, but it is possible to cope without a car – and get a girlfriend.'

we'd prefer them to use standard local bus services – but the problem is that these are deregulated and the council has no control over schedules or fares.'

Whilst most towns have seen a 40 per cent hike in traffic levels over the past twenty years, Oxford has found that due to its four park-and-ride sites congestion in the city is still not as bad as the level in 1977, even though visitor numbers are up.

On yer bike

An alternative to a mix of public transport and private driving is the non-polluting bicycle. The Cyclists' Touring Club (CTC), set up in 1878, was Britain's first road-user group. 'It was started when cycling was new and growing, and people were quite scared of bicycles,' says Colin Graham from the Policy and Planning Department at CTC's Godalming office. As cyclists became inferior citizens CTC has had to fight to keep cycles on the road. In the UK only 2.3 per cent of journeys are made by bike, whereas in Denmark it's 18.4 per cent and in the Netherlands a whopping 27.3 per cent.[7] Besides lobbying the government the group organizes National Bike Week every June – which is marked in myriad ways, from short bike rides to cyclists meeting for breakfast celebrations at Colchester.

'That's a positive mass demonstration which attracts a quarter of a million people,' says Graham, who has used his pedal passion to secure £12 million for a cycle network around Perth, Australia. 'We want to move away from this populist view that what cyclists want is off-road provision. A cycle lane is not a strip of tarmac going nowhere,' he adds. 'We know that most journeys are under five miles, ideal for cycling, and we already have a road network which is door-to-door. Some journeys are just not appropriate by car. People shouldn't have to cycle all the time – but when they do, what we need are roads which are safer for bicycles.'

Potential cyclists need to pick where they live carefully: few fair-weather cyclists are fans of steep hills, unless they have excellent gearing. They may also need to consider what model they buy, as many public-transport connections are impossible, or more expensive, unless you are using a folding bike. 'Integrating a compact folding bicycle with public transport really does provide the key to sustainable transport,' claims David Henshaw, editor of *The Folder*, a magazine devoted to public-transport-friendly folding bicycles.[8] For shorter journeys, bikes fitted with a trailer can also be used to lug considerable loads.

Ring of bright steel

If anyone needs convincing about the levels of pollution caused by cars, they should take a train to Liverpool Street Station in London. After the IRA bomb here on 24 April 1993, a heavily policed 'Ring of Steel' was introduced to some of the oldest parts of the capital. Although the checkpoints delay car drivers, air pollution has dropped by 18 per cent – as the Corporation of London has been quick to point out. 'The initial impetus for this was security not the environment,' says Judith Mayhew, who is head of the Corporation of London's most powerful planning committee. But she admits: 'What the Ring of Steel has given us is the environmental zone we had planned to bring about over a 25-year period.'[9] The Square Mile may not yet be pedestrianized but, as the jams clear, the particulates settle and the kerbside diffusers are read, it is clear that less traffic makes the City a better, cleaner place to be.

Cars and global warming

Road traffic is a key cause of climate-altering global warming – the predicted increase in temperature world-wide due to increasing levels of greenhouse gases, such as carbon dioxide (CO_2). Although scientists are uncertain about the effects of global warming it may see sea levels rise, flooding low-lying land and drastically changing traditional weather patterns.

Because the average runaround car will pump out thirty-five tons of CO_2 during its life,[10] you only have to multiply that by the number of cars in the world to see why traffic is such a serious headache.

The good news is that by 2025 scientists expect life-threatening exhaust emissions to be cut by about a third as the car industry devises more efficient engines, lightweight construction and improved design.[11] However, because by then there will have been a massive increase in private car ownership, any environmental gains will have been cancelled out.

It's traffic pollution which is top of most people's worry list. In a recent survey 65 per cent of the respondents said traffic pollution caused them a 'fair amount' of worry, way ahead of other twentieth-century *fin de siècle* nuisances – drugs, violent attacks and food safety.[12] And no wonder, as even the government admits that air pollution – much of it from vehicle exhaust fumes – kills up to twenty-four thousand people each year in Britain.[13]

The number of deaths on the road is a fraction of the number made ill by air pollution from vehicle exhausts. Nowadays one in seven children has asthma, which means that an average school has four sufferers per class. Recently a survey found that eight out of ten asthma sufferers are made worse by pollution from cars. 'For these people life is a daily struggle,' says Melinda Letts, chief executive of the National Asthma Campaign. 'People with asthma suffer in an economy which places more importance on the motor car than people's health.' As it is, alleviating asthma costs the UK £500 million in prescription charges each year.

Thanks to the car, Brits walk 20 per cent less than they did twenty years ago, and cycle 25 per cent less. Kids are most likely to suffer, especially seven-to-nine-year-olds, because parents fear to let them out on the streets unsupervised. The decline in walking for the eleven-to-fifteen age group is around 28 per cent.[14]

Not only does reliance on the car make kids less fit, it also increases the traffic, especially around schools, which is making the roads too dangerous to walk or cycle to school in the first place.[15] Even the Minister for London Transport, Glenda Jackson, calls this trend 'a cause for concern'.[16]

Bizarrely, many people say they would *cut down* on exercise if they stopped using their car: 24 per cent would watch or participate in sport less often and 7 per cent would give it up altogether.[17] It makes you wonder what they think sport is, given that doctors say walking is one of the best forms of exercise. Sharp, the national forum for coronary heart disease prevention, claims that regular cyclists enjoy a fitness level equal to that of a non-cyclist ten years younger.[18]

Mind that child

In 1971, 80 per cent of seven-to-eight-year-olds went to school unaccompanied by an adult. By 1990 this was down to just 9 per cent – and the main reason parents gave for their insistence on driving the kids to school, or chaperoning them, was fear of traffic.[19] If parents hadn't worked out the traffic demons themselves, they were alerted by public-safety campaigns urging parents to keep toddlers on reins, and stressing the need to accompany all children under twelve years old. The kids were drilled during school hours too with the Green Cross Code.

When the Royal Society for the Prevention of Accidents (RoSPA) Road Safety Division found that half the children involved in accidents were unaccompanied they concluded that parents were 'shirking their responsibilities by letting the children out alone'. But what kind of a life do children have who aren't allowed out to play, especially if they live in flats with no garden? Colin Ward's book *The Child in the City* points out that 'The children who are most at risk from the car in the city are those who have least access to its benefit.'[20]

Even those who don't have kids feel the presence of the car in every town around 8.30 a.m. and 3.30 p.m. when the roads clog up with the school-run mums. Mums who daren't let their children walk to school in case they're hit by cars – or attacked by the 1990s street devil, the child molester. According to the Royal Commission on Environmental Pollution, 20 per cent of peak-time road journeys are school runs.

But things are changing. There are now schools where parents hire a minibus, or 'police' their children's walking routes to school, or campaign for one-way systems to help ease the polluting gridlock. The private girls' Royal School, in Hampstead, has managed to slash its going-home traffic. The school's bursar wrote to parents of the 202 pupils urging them to pool car journeys or trade in big vehicles for smaller as part of its policy to show the local authority, Camden, that it could cut traffic and could therefore be trusted to expand.[21] Their simple success ended up being praised in a *Times* editorial: 'Schools appear indifferent to the problems of parking, traffic control and pollution. But what they and parents now believe is that walking to school, even if possible is unwise . . . Encouragingly parents and some schools are now volunteering time and money to cut the morning crush . . . Private schools are the pioneers . . . but state schools too must tackle the traffic. Safety at school is paramount, but so is getting there safely, healthily and on time.'[22]

Sticking to it

However, it isn't always easy to maintain temporary travel changes, as villagers at Claygate, in Surrey, have found. 'The Claygate Village Residents Association has been running a campaign to try to encourage local schools to put pressure on parents and allow their children to walk to school,' says the chairman Brian Rhodes. 'During Walk to School Week in June we reduced cars by 40 per cent, but now it's winter it's back to normal and there's 101 excuses.'

After doing their sums the residents calculated that the 4500 on the electoral roll owned around 3000 cars – twice as many as twenty years ago. This inspired the Residents Association to embark on a Claygate for the People campaign, to encourage residents to become less dependent on the motor car and to improve the way of life in the village. 'The official speed limit is 30 mph but not many people keep to it, preferring speeds of over 40 mph on roads designed for the horse and trap,' says Rhodes. 'So we designed a car sticker urging residents to keep at 25 mph through Claygate.' These have been distributed at the flower show and the association's AGM, and posted through more than nine hundred letterboxes. 'It makes a difference.

I travel dutifully at 25 mph and find that I get no hassle from drivers behind because people see the sticker. However, it is a struggle to persuade people to drive more slowly, even in their own village,' adds Rhodes. 'What we really need is a reduction in the national speed limit to 25 mph in built-up areas. The current limit was fixed well over sixty years ago, when traffic on the roads was negligible and most cars could not travel more than 50 mph in any case.'

Sometimes local groups campaigning for traffic changes can face legal problems. For example a local residents group in Kingston-upon-Thames was so angry when the local council decided to overturn the Neighbourhood Committee's unanimous vote to close two roads to through traffic that it is seeking a judicial review. Dogged persistence and successful test cases, combined with legislative change on the home-zone front, may yet help bring about a major change in the way we live and our children play.

Lynn Sloman, assistant director at Transport 2000, points out that 'Councils aren't powerless. OK, the council can't give home zones, which is why Transport 2000 is running a campaign, but if residents want traffic-calming or less traffic or safe crossings outside a school, or a road closed to traffic, the local authority does have the power to do it. The first thing to do is work out who else in your area has a similar agenda and turn an issue to traffic-calm one street into something bigger, so it becomes an issue for the whole town.'

Sloman also stresses the need for campaigners to use their imagination. 'It's very easy to be sucked into making polite presentations at meetings – but unless you kick up a fuss the council won't sort a problem out. You need to play by *your* rules and to use the media and stunts. Be creative and humorous to keep people on-side and attract the media, but don't be too heavy.'

Sloman campaigns in the streets near her home too. After ten years of local groups asking for a zebra crossing to make access to Finsbury Park tube and rail station safer, nothing had happened. So a group of locals, each dressed in either black or white, went to their chosen spot and lay down in the road to make a human zebra crossing. Less than twelve months later the council installed the crossing. She also points out that there's no need to get disheartened if your group of committed organizers seems very small. 'Even if there's only five of you, or just one of you, there is a group of people out there who will pitch up at larger events. What you've got to do is keep them informed through community newsletters or by leaflets. But you can also get in touch with other community groups, and that's why Transport 2000 set up the Streets For People network. Half the battle is knowing that you're not on your own – you don't need to invent everything from scratch.'

For example, in Leeds the residents of Methley Terrace turfed over a hundred-yard stretch for the weekend so that they could hold a summer fête, on a road normally used as a rat run. For three days in September 1996 kids could play football safely, residents sunbathe without being choked by fumes, and chatting neighbours hear each other's reply. Despite a BBC camera crew searching for voices of dissent, even the terrace's resident Mr Angry admitted, 'I'd like this grass to be permanent. I thought this road plan would be a bit of a ridiculous thing to do. They've done a good job.'[23]

Even if rat runs can't be permanently stopped, drivers can be made to slow down. One tried and tested method is traffic-calming. The first traffic-calming in the country was tried out in

Hertfordshire at Buntingford, a historic ribbon of houses and shops fronting the ancient Roman road, Hare Street; and then implemented in Borehamwood and Stanstead Abbots. Yet although it has successfully slowed traffic in many towns, emotions are still mixed about its introduction. People feel it messes up their suspension, whilst glaziers have even more trouble. However, a local councillor pointed out the council's logic: 'Until speed limits in residential areas can be reduced to 20 mph and driver behaviour moderated in relation to speed limits and other traffic laws, traffic-calming schemes are the best means of reducing accidents.' Put another way, if a car hits a pedestrian at 20 mph then only one in twenty is killed. If the car is going at 30 mph, nearly half will be killed and at 40 mph nearly all will be killed.[24]

Party zone

Car-free streets are also becoming synonymous with summer celebrations. Edinburgh Festival now sees the Royal Mile turn into a pedestrians-only area for three weeks each August. In London the A1 red route through Upper Street has a day off for Islington's summerfest; as does Church Street for the Stoke Newington festival, and the whole of Notting Hill Gate during the carnival. The Lord Mayor's Show also gives the City of London an annual rest from traffic. People are even starting to think about giving town centres back to the pedestrian – the critical test for the roads lobby will be if London's Trafalgar Square can be transformed into a traffic no-go area.

As well as holding the Fuming Mad Rally in Trafalgar Square, transport campaigners have been trying to raise awareness about the possibilities of us all using our cars less by highlighting Local Transport Day and, more recently, the more racy National Car-Free Day.

In 1996 Brighton shoppers signed a pledge that they would leave their cars at home for two days out of every seven; in Lancaster a conference was held which concluded that council officials should use bikes rather than cars, every residential street should have traffic-calming, some streets should be car-free and targets should be set for reducing traffic in Lancaster and Morecambe by 35 per cent by 2005;[25] whilst in Leicester John Pochin from Barkby showed off his battery-powered Fiesta with its top speed of 50 mph. The conversion saves him £790 in running costs each year – and is somewhat kinder to the environment than the petrol-powered model.[26]

The same year FoE ran Curb the Car Day, which attracted support from Zoë Ball, Anna Friel and the cast of *Byker Grove*. Highlights – besides trying to persuade people to leave their car at home on Sunday 30 June – included campaigners handing out bottles of 'fresh air' and slapping parking tickets on cars.

Honesty box

'There has been a sea change,' says Kerry Hamilton, Professor of Transport at the University of East London. 'At a conference where I was giving a paper on transport and health to some well-heeled doctors, they'd circulated a questionnaire asking, "How did you get here?" The choices included "car", "car – on my own", "bus", "walk" and so on. At the bottom it said, "Please be honest." Five years ago, of course the delegates would have come on their own in their car! Now they're asked to be honest about driving on their own in a car, the penny's dropped.' What's clear is that you are never too old to make a difference. And individuals are recognizing this.

Mid-life car critic

'I drove as soon as I could,' says Simon Baddeley, who teaches

politics and management at Birmingham University; he is fifty-five and a little portly. Although he does not admit to a mid-life crisis, a time when it's not unknown for men to splash out on a sports car, Baddeley has engineered a lifestyle shake-up by converting to pedal power.

'I've still got a car parked in the drive. It's a Montego estate, the most boring car in the world, but since I've started cycling to work more often I don't really enjoy getting into it. I think, Oh, God! Where will I park it? I still have lots of happy memories of car journeys but now motoring just bores me.

'I've been edging towards being Greener for some time,' he continues, 'after thinking about the wicked problems, roads, cars, lack of green spaces in the city . . . Then two years ago the Newbury Bypass went through Bagnor village, where I used to live. That got me thinking even more about traffic and congestion.' Baddeley wrote letters of complaint to MPs and took part in peaceful demonstrations, with little effect, but now he feels he's found a way to stop being part of the UK's traffic problem: he uses his car less.

Already he's determined to show there are benefits from giving up driving. He is one of 120 people who have volunteered as cycling guinea pigs for a joint project run by Birmingham University's sports lab and the city council's Transportation Department. First task was to have a physical examination so the researchers can calculate if there are any health improvements for middle-aged people who cycle regularly. The next was to get on the bike. 'The understanding is that I must cycle two days a week. But I find the twelve-mile journey to and from work along the canal is wonderful, it makes commuting a bit of an adventure. Nowadays I grumble about motorists and am finding that the cycling experience has put me through a mental shift. I am horrified by the way people drive.

They go too fast, they drive through red lights – and half of them look like me.'

A few months before he pumped up his tyres and took to cycling seriously, Baddeley had a near miss with a young girl who collided with the side of his car on a back street. *'Luckily I was going about 15 mph, but if I'd been going at the speed allowed, 30 mph, then although I wouldn't have been blamed I'm sure she would have been dead,' he recalls. This experience got him thinking. 'I added up the number of people I knew well who had been killed in car or motor-bike crashes over the past fifty years. It was six. Finally the statistics about safety came home: I can see what a lethal piece of machinery a car is. I do still use the Montego, but I'm changing my driving habits. There's a real art to driving safely – it's much more difficult than the driving test implies. You have to be as skilled as an airline pilot.'*

Despite his proselytizing, his sixteen-year-old son can't wait to drive his own car. *'He thinks I'm a bit pathetic,' laughs Baddeley; 'he sees cars as a way to leave home. And my wife can't imagine getting rid of her car because of the papers she has to take to and from work. I understand that, but there is a danger that I'm going to turn into a whinger, when really I just want to enjoy using my bicycle safely on the roads.'*

Divorce broke Susan Hoyle's driving habit. 'I'd had a car for ten years, but with the break-up I just couldn't afford one.' A few years later her new partner decided to give up his car too. Despite the pair having four kids they reckoned a car-free existence wouldn't be a problem in London. And they were right.

'One of the great benefits was we didn't spend our children's teenage years ferrying them around,' reckons Susan. 'Not having a car also saved us over £3000 a year. We did spend money on taxis, including a weekly trip back from Sainsbury's.' Most other local trips were by public transport, or foot. Then in 1990 Susan bought a sturdy fold-up bike, which could be taken on trains for free, and which so impressed her partner that he bought another the next day!

'Life is different without a car,' she admits. 'You need to plan ahead, for example if you are going to catch trains, and you need to be more disciplined about how much luggage you take.'

Twelve years since they said goodbye to their car, the pair have reluctantly bought a van. 'It's to help my son, who's a drummer, as even I can't see how you can carry a drumkit without four wheels. Over the past five weeks I've only made two trips in it, and one was to a garden centre which wouldn't deliver,' says Susan. 'I hadn't realized cars were so inconvenient. It takes so much longer getting around in a van than cycling. Sitting in the front passenger seat also feels uncomfortable. I feel I ought to be doing something – on a train I'd get on with work, and cycling is good exercise as well as fun. But sitting in the van is just a waste of time.'

There's also the problem of finding a place to park near your home. For those without off-street parking or a garage, the solution is a wheelie bin or plants on buckets. 'Living here has just become a nightmare,' says Fiona Duff, who used to like Clapham South. 'Everyone in the street is putting out their bins and we are looking out of the window all the time. If things don't get better, we're just going to have to move.'

CHAPTER NINE

The highwaymen business

'Most people don't learn to drive, they learn to pass the driving test,' says Bryan Lunn, chief examiner at the Institute of Advanced Motorists. IAM was set up in 1954 and has around 107,000 members who have passed its demanding test, which is based on police driving skills. But it is worth it: members' chances of causing an accident are sharply reduced – one survey reckoned they were 75 per cent less likely to be involved in an accident.[1]

Each month about a thousand people apply to take the test, which Lunn feels is far too few. 'There are more than thirty million drivers on our roads and most people seem to think they are pretty damn good at driving. But we're killing 3500 people every year, so our driving cannot be called good.'

IAM reckon that 95 per cent of accidents are due to driver failure, and feel industry safety improvements are a red herring. 'It's all very well having traffic-calming and manufacturers building in airbags and bumper crumple zones, but the component that keeps failing is the driver. There's no such thing as a dangerous road. People go too fast in the wrong places. No one has the right to drive badly,' says Lunn, a former policeman, who despairs of the people he encounters daily on the roads during his commute from Essex to Chiswick. 'Good driving takes place in the brain; it's not just about kicking pedals. You need concentration, observation, anticipation, planning and good handling skills. Get the driver right and you get road safety right.'

Strop gear

But road safety is not what the avid watchers of Britain's top car programme on TV want to be lectured about – they want to know how cars perform. *Top Gear* regularly attracts audiences of four million, ensuring it remains as one of BBC2's flagship programmes. But many people also feel that the presenters set a bad example through their incorrigible love of speed. Indeed, Jeremy Clarkson's (the best known of the *Top Gear* team) love of fast motors has led to spin-off columns in the *Sun* and the *Sunday Times* and two best-selling books, *Clarkson on Cars* and the more recent *Hot 100: Cars That Make You Go Phwoar!*. Here Clarkson drools over vehicles for their speed, looks, pull potential and iconic status. And the faster they go the better – like Clarkson's own red Ferrari 355, which stars on the book's front cover and which offers a top temptation of 183 mph, which Clarkson is willing to bust . . . 'And at that point, it's screaming the sort of scream that makes you think a large dog has got stuck in the jaws of an even larger shark. And you are doing 155 mph. And then you are slotting the gear lever through its open gate into sixth, heading for 185 or, if the wind is with you, a little more.'[2]

'It's an awful programme,' says one viewer, Di Whitefield, who taught her two eldest daughters to drive and passed an advanced driver's test in 1996: 'far too geared up around speed. Today what you need are cars which are fun to drive and don't go so fast. One of the basic rules of driving is to hold on to the steering wheel, but in *Top Gear* the presenters are often seen swinging their hands across the wheel, or worse, driving with one hand so they can gesticulate with the other – as if they can't talk and drive with two hands.'

Bryan Lunn's colleague at IAM, Ted Clements, complains: 'The worst of the programme is knowing that the participants don't want to change their driving style at all.'

Clarkson is repeatedly singled out for his boy-racer attitudes. On a recent *Right to Reply*, clips of him grinning as he took the £50,000 XJR above 100 mph and announcing it was 'bonkers fast . . . rockets nought to sixty in five seconds' were shown to demonstrate why viewer Suzanne Lockyer, from Leicestershire, thinks *Top Gear* is irresponsible. She managed to interview the aptly named John Bentley, editor of the BBC's motoring and leisure-sports programmes, who claimed *Top Gear* wasn't glamorizing speed. 'I wouldn't want viewers to emulate driving fast on public roads . . . [but we've got to] face the facts that every car on sale in Great Britain is capable of exceeding all speed limits . . . It's down to individual drivers' responsibility to make sure they don't.'

Lockyer, a very neat-looking woman with no evidence of facial hair or slogan-draped T-shirts, then asked if the government's Kill Your Speed campaign would have an effect on the programme's contents, only to be fobbed off by Bentley saying: 'The campaign may have factors which impinge on the car and car use . . . but we've always looked at environmental aspects and safety aspects of cars.' No wonder Lockyer, who admits she loves her car but thinks it's time for drivers to practise speed restraint, exasperatedly turned to camera to ask: 'When there's so much talk about banning guns and drugs and smoking I can't believe TV is still allowed to portray one of society's most lethal weapons in this way.'[3]

Roadcraft

Keeping your eyes on the road and your hands on the steering wheel are basic rules, but how many times have you read a map, scrabbled around for a tape or even used a mobile phone on the move? A recent study by RoSPA has found that hand-held phones are dangerous, but hands-free phones are also distracting, especially for drivers with manual gears. A Canadian study found that all phones affect a driver's ability to concentrate on controlling their vehicle and that mobiles are more distracting than tuning a car radio or talking to a passenger. It also found that drivers were four times more likely to have an accident during, and up to five minutes after, a conversation.[4]

Police can arrest drivers for using their mobile. But when traffic cops had a clampdown on mobile use in Colombia they were rather startled to find that two-thirds of the people stopped for 'using' their carphones did not have a phone that worked – they were just showing off to other road users. And it works: bizarrely, researchers have also found that drivers spotting someone on their mobile makes more than half see red, further increasing the possibility of a crash.[5]

Buying cars

As car ownership gets more and more widespread, it seems that fewer people make the effort to find out the basics about how they work. Some don't even bother to check the oil, haven't a clue where the anti-freeze goes and are at a loss about why tyres need to be at the recommended pressure. Because so few people are confident under a bonnet, membership of a motoring organization is an essential part of car ownership. But as cars become increasingly computerized knowing basic mechanics may no longer matter.

'It's very dispiriting the way people buy used cars,' says Luke Boslett at the AA; 'they seem to spend more time choosing their holiday than on the car which is going to carry them about the roads for the next three years.' During a day out with AA patrolman Frank Moorby I was astounded by how few people knew anything about the way their cars worked.

On the road with an AA patrolman

In the cavernous Lancaster Forte Posthouse there's a bar, two dining rooms, and nothing much for the travelling salesmen to do except drink, dine and mouth along to the cheesy tunes. No one has anything in common – except how we arrived. At Reception they may ask for your name first, but they want to know your car's details too. This car-oriented hotel seems an appropriate place to meet up with an AA patrol.

'The weather predicts our workload,' explains Frank as he meets me in the hotel's car park. 'Bad weather keeps us busy.' Frank should know: he's worked for the AA for twenty years in one of the areas of Britain that sees a lot of weather. When the sun's out it's a truly beautiful region, offering views of Cornforth Station, where much of the classic romantic movie Brief Encounter *was filmed; the Lakes; the long seafront of Morecambe, where he lives; the castled hilltop city of Lancaster; and the moors, which afford a panoramic view over the region from Blackpool to the Lakes. When the weather's bad it's a job even to see the road.*

On average Frank will do six jobs per day in his Leyland Daf 400 van. If it's frosty that'll include fixing flat batteries, and if it's wet and windy contending with the elements as much as the mechanical challenges. 'Rain is the worst, as soon as you lift the bonnet the engine gets flooded,' he says. But good weather brings its own troubles too – overheating engines and holidaymakers in badly maintained cars. Over the past two years he's clocked up forty-three thousand miles on patrol duty. Boredom can be a problem. 'You get used to waiting for a job,' says Frank, driving towards Morecambe. 'I park up and the time goes. In my first week I thought I'd pack it up, but then I found that you don't get many quiet days.'

For a while we sit in the sunny cab, watching the tide shift the mud of the bay. After only minutes the mobile data terminal flashes up a job. He's got to find a Nissan Sunny that's cut out near by. The control centre has budgeted twelve minutes for Frank to get there, and another twenty for the repair. In fact the broken-down car is very close and we reach it in half that time – as we pull up Frank sums up the situation whilst passing me a reflective waistcoat. 'He's a window cleaner,' he announces as the ladder on the roof gives its owner's occupation away. It's a locally based member and, as the car is already booked for attention at a garage near by, Frank tows it to Kwik Fit, and then drops the window cleaner back home.

Within half an hour he is free for the next job. AA patrols meet every type of driver. Frank has towed a car converted into a large clown, used to promote events in Blackpool, down the motorway to Stoke-on-Trent just for a photo session; he's met most of the absent-minded shoppers who've locked their keys in the car during a trip to Sainsbury's; and has plenty of times reached a broken-down vehicle on the motorway before its owner has tramped back from the emergency phonebox. He's also helped the odd Land-Rover out of a muddy field on the few occasions a farmer has put the wrong tyres on.

Everyone has an AA story: people who've managed to lock their keys into a car after changing into swimming gear for a winter dip in Bournemouth; people who've broken down a few miles inside the Cornish border – where they'd planned to have a holiday – but have to be towed all the way back to their starting point with the relay service; people in full wedding gear who got a guided tour of Oxford after their car broke down on the M40; and people who've been willing to tamper with their car so it breaks down on the long haul from Scotland to London to get a tow back to their home, again with the relay policy. It's the organization's familiarity, the way we can swap breakdown tales and the hours waiting on the hard shoulder in the pub, which enables it to call itself 'the fourth emergency service'. A well-known set of TV ads has also ensured that people still greet the patrol's arrival with the catchphrase 'He's a very nice man' – even though the AA does now employ women too.

'I just play along with it,' admits Frank – who's been greeted that way more times than he remembers – punching in the codes that signal the end of the job; 'it's all about keeping members happy.'

Twelve noon: a job's come in for a Ford Transit which has lost all acceleration on the M6. When we reach the rather tatty van, which is being used to collect second-hand clothes in Lancaster and drop them in Manchester, it takes Frank just two minutes to fix, after seeing that the throttle linkage has come adrift.

'If drivers explain the problem right you can usually fix it. First you need to know the vehicle's history, then find out the signs – such as what's happened before – and then find out the symptoms: that's when they tell you how the vehicle cut out. I learnt that twenty years ago and it still works,' says Frank, clearly disappointed that the jobs so far haven't tested his mechanical skills in any way.

The next job isn't much of a challenge either: a doctor has locked his car keys into the boot in a car park back in Lancaster.

We are late arriving, as the AA is no longer allowed to use the works bridge to shorten the M6; instead we drive nearly to the Preston turn-off before we can double back to Lancaster. Unfortunately the car has central locking and electronic deadlock and is not prepared to let itself be tricked into opening with a fishing line or a rubber doorstop.

Whilst Frank calls up the central office to check on tactics for this particular Vauxhall Vectra, the psychologist starts to panic about his next appointment and turns his mobile red hot. Short of forcing in the sunroof and then battering down the boot divide, there's nothing that can be done – the easiest option is for the doctor to track down his wife and get her to drive over with the spare key. It means another half-hour wait and so Frank parks and turns up the heater to unfreeze the doctor, who's already spent a cold half-hour waiting for us to arrive, until his wife turns up. 'She doesn't know the area well,' says the doctor, looking at the crossroads anxiously, 'but we have the AA in South Africa, with the same yellow vans, so she'll recognize you.'

While we wait for the keys Frank recounts unlocking tales. He reckons that most older cars can be unlocked in two or three minutes. 'I was called out to help an old lady who'd locked her keys inside in Boots' car park. It took me five minutes to break in – and when she realized how easy it was she told me she was sending the car back! But with these computer-designed cars it's harder; sometimes you need power in the battery to be able to unlock the car, which is fine until the battery goes flat.'

By now it's close to half-one and Frank wants a break. Half an hour later we head off to the hills and wild country of Quernmore at Jubilee Tower. The roads here are tiny and windy and see a fair share of breakdowns, but it's clearly a quiet day today. 'There's a lot of breakdowns up here, but I come to look *at the view too. When I drive up here I feel so relaxed. Maybe it's because I'm not local [he was born in Motherwell, once famous for its ironworks, but now better known for car auctions] so I appreciate it more. And when it's snowing on those hills everything stands out. It's beautiful, but it's difficult to explain,' he says. 'I'd sooner be working up in the hills than down on the motorway, motorways are so monotonous.'*

There's a beep and the data terminal flashes up travel information: police have cordoned off Blackpool because of a suspected bomb.

We pull over and Frank signals for me to have a look at a small tourist plaque for the Quernmore Burial, which was discovered when a gravel car park was put in during the seventies for visitors to the tower. And then another job comes in, and it's back to the motorway. The only clue that this is still a rural area comes when we see a herd of dairy cows crossing a farm bridge over the M6 on their way to milking.

As we pull up by the G-reg car, Frank sees he's in for trouble: there's a large puddle of oil on the ground under it. On the side of the road are five children and three adults waiting for help. 'Don't say this job's not exciting,' says Frank, sending the overexcited kids to his cab to warm up. The eldest girl, eleven-year-old Samantha, fills me in on the details of the family's life – they have been in Scotland, her dad is a taxi driver, the hired car has broken down, she's from Wales, her friends are going to Bootle in Liverpool, and she has a dog – while Frank hitches up the car and tows it off the motorway because the engine has blown up and dropped all its oil. There he arranges for another AA driver to tow the car and its occupants back to their respective homes.

'You're not allowed to use a mobile and drive are you?' says Samantha imperiously, clearly enjoying her mum's

misadventure as she watches Frank organizing the next set of transport on his mobile. 'It's illegal isn't it? A man drove into our Sierra last year, but we've still got it. Did I tell you we have a dog?'

'Not many members get angry,' says Frank after the arrangements are finalized. 'You can understand people getting mad,' he agrees, 'because it's their vehicle which has broken down, and it can be expensive, but they are the lucky ones, they're AA members.'

Frank may have shown himself to be the archetypal AA knight of the road – he's polite, warm, friendly and skilled with people and cars – but the jobs haven't challenged him enough. 'Today was a bit disappointing,' he admits: 'usually there's more fixing of cars; spare keys are usually hundreds of miles away, rather than twenty minutes; and I've never dealt with a big family like that. If we'd got that last job in the morning we'd have taken the car over to north Wales. I used to do a lot of relay, some years I'd drive sixty or seventy thousand miles. But when it comes down to it I prefer getting vehicles running again – and that's about imagination as much as the flair to repair.'

Bitter struggle

As drivers are painfully aware, it's not usually a broken fanbelt that stops you getting to your meeting or your holiday destination, it's more likely to be a massive traffic jam on the M25. This is where new technology may bolster the fortunes of both the car industry – because global-positioning gadgets can cost – and the motoring organizations – because they can provide flying-eye-style information about road conditions and suggest alternative routes. As a result there is a bitter struggle going on within the rescue organizations as to where to position themselves for future business. Both the RAC and AA are putting faith in the role that telematics, the information services which keep drivers up to date about traffic routes, will play, but that's where the similarities seem to end.

'The AA is reverting to type,' claims Jeremy Vanke, who is head of public policy at the RAC and until seven years ago was a campaigner at Friends of the Earth. 'They're consciously becoming pro-motorist and sod the consequences.' As evidence he points to a news item in *Auto Express*, where the AA's head of roads and transportation policy, Paul Walters, says: 'Some may think we've failed our members in recent times. But we're swinging back in favour of the motorist. Expect us to take a much more active stance.'[6]

How did this battle line develop? Vanke claims the RAC's approach, dismissed as mere greenwash by the cynics, has been tempered by acceptance that you 'can't build enough roads to cater for forecast traffic growth, so that takes you into different policies. To manage congestion there will be times when motorists have to leave their cars at home. But to do that, there has to be choice.

'There is no one solution, or technical panacea, when it comes to vehicle pollution. We can all make improvements but it needs to be combined with improved public transport, walking, cycling and telematics,' Vanke adds. 'What's going to have to be done will appear to be relatively small changes, but will have the sum greater than its parts.' He admits this is going to require selflessness from drivers, but insists, 'In the long term it's in their interests, because if changes aren't made there will be sticks like road-pricing – although that may be useful if the money raised is used to improve transport generally.'

Both the AA and the RAC are members of the British Roads Federation, which has not yet given up actively lobbying government for more roads. Green Flag, another membership organization which provides rescue services, is guilty too, in that its parent company, NCP, is a BRF member. That's why some people turn to the newest of these member organizations for breakdown support, the Environmental Transport Association (ETA). ETA was set up by transport campaigners in 1990 and positively oozes Green credentials. It now has fifteen thousand members. As well as providing a breakdown service and Britain's first recovery service for cyclists, it co-ordinates the annual Green Transport Week and Car-Free Day.

Good company

But the group which look set to have the biggest problems changing their behaviour are the company-car drivers. Companies in the UK own around 2.3 million cars, and half of the cars on the roads have at some time been company-owned.[7] That's why the companies' car-purchase policies have such an impact. In general company cars tend to be larger-engined models, making them more expensive to run. They also cover around twice the mileage of private cars, a total of forty-five billion miles a year, so they have a significant impact on both the environment and road congestion.[8] On the plus side, company cars are often newer and better-maintained than private vehicles, which means they have lower emissions of pollutants.

But the problem for many companies is that, however willing they are in principle to do what's best for the environment, the choices are limited by commercial pressures. The Royal Mail, which delivers to twenty-six million addresses daily, feels this acutely. 'We are obliged to deliver mail quickly and efficiently and at the moment we have a diesel fleet, supported by bikes, nationwide railway and aircraft. If there was a product which was extremely environmentally friendly we would use it. But electric vehicles do not have the speed or distance capabilities. There is immense time pressure,' says Angus Thomson. 'As a driver I never think about the pollutant value of my car but when you have got twenty-nine thousand diesel engines you have to be responsible and think long and hard. But diesel engines have served us well and we would only part with them if something better came along.'

The problem with using diesel engines, even in new vehicles, is that they produce more particulates and nitrogen oxides (NO_x), including nitric oxide, nitrogen dioxide and nitrous oxide, than a vehicle using petrol. Both particulates and NO_x have a detrimental effect on people's health, particularly in car-choked urban areas.

Currently the Royal Mail is experimenting, not with petrol, but with a range of liquefied gases, including propane, with Ford-made vans working in the Croydon area. 'It's not intended to make a difference in its own right, it's a trial,' explains Thomson. However, the company has put considerable effort into improving drivers' skills. 'We're very high profile, and very noticeable because our vehicles are bright red with yellow markings, so we want to be noticeable for our excellence,' he says. Indeed the Royal Mail has a reputation as having a thorough internal driving training programme, although it was reluctant to provide any indication of how much is actually spent.

The AA, which has a fleet of five thousand vehicles clocking up around 125 million miles a year, insists all drivers of a company vehicle must take a one-day course in defensive driving. This course aims to improve fuel efficiency and reduce accidents, maintenance and tyre wear – and it costs less than 10p per day for each driver. And it's money well spent, as

RoSPA claims that defensive driver training cuts accident rates by up to 70 per cent in two years.

Fuel gauge eyes

Car dealers are obliged by law to provide fuel-consumption figures for new models. Usually two figures are supplied, one for a constant cruise speed of 56 mph and one for stop–start conditions in town traffic. However, few drivers are able to match these figures in actual conditions. This may be because they are on the road with a cold engine, or in bad weather, or in a hurry, or with a poorly tuned or heavily loaded car. Automatic transmission can add between 10 and 15 per cent to fuel consumption, even if the owner puts the car into neutral at traffic lights and brief stops. On all cars sudden acceleration or braking also gobbles up fuel. However, this doesn't explain why some drivers use 30 per cent more fuel than others – making air quality that much worse.[9]

Although driver training is expensive, fuel-efficient driving, which adds 10 mpg per car in a fifty-vehicle fleet, can enable companies to slash bills. For example, if each car was driven an average of twenty thousand miles, fuel costs could drop by £15,000.[10] That's why the best-managed fleets use half as much fuel as the worst.[11]

Even so the miles-per-gallon rate is rarely a high priority for someone buying a car – and it's even less of one for most company-car drivers, especially if they do not have to pay for the fuel they use. The poshest cars, like Bentleys and Rolls-Royces, tend to have very high mpg consumption. Early American models were well known for their gas-guzzling tendencies: a 1956 Cadillac only managed twelve miles to the gallon.

One way to encourage better fuel efficiency take-up rates was found during a survey by researchers from the Monks

Partnership. This showed that companies offering a cash incentive to employees if they switched to a more fuel-efficient car could work, when the average incentive was between 30 and 80 per cent of the company's own cost saving. However, Monks warned: 'It is important to sell the message effectively . . . Avoid asking staff to trade down. Instead focus on the clear financial and environmental benefits of switching to a more fuel-efficient vehicle.'[12]

This is a tough command. All too often, what drivers really, really want is their climb up the management hierarchy visually marked with a snazzy company car – even a Mondeo will do if that's all on offer. As a result Monks found that more than a quarter of companies with fleets provide more status cars than business-needs cars. For example NatWest has a fleet of 8500 cars but just two thousand are essential for staff's work. Similarly at Sainsbury's, which has a fleet of 1800 vehicles, only 520 are needed to perform the job. The sheer extravagance of such a policy can even lead other company-car drivers into rage about the jams on roads caused by people who don't *have* to drive to work, but can't resist the posh-car perk. What logic rewards the best-paid employees with a free car, when they could well afford their own? And what logic is going to help turn this approach around so that company fleets in the future are dominated by fuel-efficient models, used only by people who need a car for their work?

The driver's view

Doug Anthony is based in Sussex but he needs to drive all round the country for his job. 'I have a Rover 2l fuel injection which is probably as inefficient on fuel as you can get. But because I do such a high mileage – at least two thousand miles a month – I wanted a car with get up and go.' Yet despite his choice of car

he repeatedly finds himself crawling along with the commuters.
'When I think about how to reduce cars on the roads I wonder
why people don't share cars or why the road tax isn't higher or
why more lorries don't drive at night. But I don't class myself as
a driver who can be removed from the road, the ones who could
be reduced are the people who make the same journey every
day. I see them on the A23 going to Croydon or Brixton and
there's always one person in each car, clogging up the road and
stopping me from getting from A to B. When I go to my head
office in London I always take the train. Commuting by car is a
waste of time.'

Recently Surrey County Council, which has twenty-four
thousand employees, launched its own pilot company transport
plan amongst the Environment Department employees; but it
hopes to have fifty transport plans operating by 1999.

'Many companies want to get involved because they have on-
site parking problems. It seems to be the driving force behind
change. But these changes will only be taken seriously if equity
issues are considered. You can't have hierarchy in your
company's car park,' says Matt Beale-Collins, Surrey's
TravelWise co-ordinator. As Alistair Henderson of Unison
puts it: 'We will get nowhere with staff reducing their car
dependence if they see a row of BMWs given to senior staff.'

Green gauge

Driving better, keeping safety in mind at all times, could
make our roads safer. Given that all cars pollute, you can
never be a Green driver — but thoughtful driving can
make a major difference to the amount of pollution

your car creates. For example:

- Plan journeys in advance so that you don't have to keep stopping to recheck the route. One way to do this is to list, on a large piece of cardboard, the principal places on the route, with road number and mileage. At key changes of direction put down the new road number and all possible names which may be on the signpost, including the road's ultimate destination. Such detail may sound obsessive but can be useful, especially if you are driving abroad.
- Listen to radio traffic reports to avoid major jams.
- Fast accelerating and sudden braking drink up fuel – which causes more pollution.
- The most economic driving speed is between 30 and 45 mph. Going at 70 mph uses one-third more fuel than driving at 45–50 mph, a high cost for what may amount to a saving of only a few minutes on the overall journey.
- Keep in top gear as much as possible, but only if it's not straining the car's engine – or your control
- Try not to use a car for every journey. Can you share your car with a friend? Or can you plan what you have to do so that you can get a number of things done during one trip? Sharing the cost of a journey produces the highest number of miles per gallon.
- Ideally have a catalytic converter fitted – especially if you regularly drive on motorways.
- Make sure your car is serviced regularly, and is properly tuned, so that it always operates at its most efficient.

CHAPTER TEN

Allo, John, got a new motor?

Together, the pair of schoolgirls decide their car is going to have a red base and a yellow bonnet with matching yellow roof. Satisfied with their colour scheme, they rush off giggling to the Science Museum's next touch-me display.

The car they've playfully created has some remarkable physical similarities to three models thought up by students at Coventry School of Art and Design. The Amphicar, by Peter K. Fowler, takes its colour scheme from the mallard duck, and like a duck it can also move over land and in water – ideal for a century where global warming may cause higher sea levels. Then there's a futuristic-looking pod vehicle envisioned by John Hancock which converts from electric commuter buggy to petrol sports car by renting an alternative chassis. And there's the Auburn Speedster 851 from Mark Randall, modelled on a classic sports-car design but with an advanced engine system which makes the car more fuel-efficient and slashes harmful emissions.

The exhibition fills a tiny corner of the Science Museum and it guarantees interest, not because there's going to be a crisis if we don't design new types of car, but because it's directly between two popular pit stops: the café and the space exploration gallery. In just ten display units the Science Museum attempts to show how very different cars of the future could be. Lighter. Recyclable. Less polluting. With telematics – a kind of on-board information service about traffic conditions ahead. They'll break down less often and they'll do a lot more of the steering. And that time isn't far away. Already more than a million cars in Japan use an on-board navigational system.[1]

By the year 2000 we could all be getting good roadside routing from personal global-positioning systems. By 2007 night driving will be made safer by the use of infra-red technology, and by 2020 we can expect hands-free steering – even at speeds of 50 mph – on convoys along the motorway. It's all rather disappointing: hands-free driving has already been trialled in America, to try to control highway congestion, back in the summer of 1997. The only space-age-looking development on show at the Science Museum is a silver-coloured shuttle service, known as Personal Rapid Transport, which looks fiendishly expensive.

Some of the students visiting have written down their ideas: 'I think the car of the future should be electric to stop pollution' or 'The car of the future needs wings for speeding through the rush-hour traffic on the M25.' There's also another, disgruntled voice, and I suspect it's written by one of those schoolgirl 'engineers': 'I think it's stupid that in the year 2000 you have to be seventeen before you can drive.' Even for a generation brought up on environmental scaremongering, getting your hands on a car is still highly desirable. And the museum knows that too. In its shop it is selling two different calendars featuring classic American cars, a variety of Galt soft-toy cars for babies, and a learning game about traffic road rules, suitable for kids of six years and up.

Twenty years ago historians were fantasizing that the millennium would bring an end to the polluting, noisy world of the car. After researching *The Age of the Automobile* for Granada TV and producing a book of the same name, Harold Perkin concluded that instant personal mobility was going to change radically:

'It might take the form of a small personal hovercraft or helicopter, but these would still require petrol or a similar fuel, would still produce noise and pollution, would still require parking space, and might produce even more congestion and problems of traffic management – in the latter case of three dimensional traffic lanes. It is conceivable that some smaller device attached to the person, a powered trolley or a flying pack, could provide the same instant mobility without the problem of parking – just leave it in the cloakroom or left luggage office.'[2]

It is still hard to figure out why researchers have taken so long to come up with a blueprint for a different car when sci-fi writers have been so certain that conventional models would be museum pieces by the turn of the millennium. Dr Who used a Tardis, which could move through time and relative dimensions in space – and you certainly never saw him filling up at the local petrol station. The *Star Trek* crew used a transporter beam to shift people around, spawning the catchphrase: 'Beam me up, Scotty.' Luke Skywalker and Han Solo zoomed around in the *Millennium Falcon*, a sort of Grand Prix racing in space, without the tyre-tearing trouble.

The American engineer and architect Buckminster Fuller, perhaps better known for the development of the geodesic dome and his book *Operating Manual for Spaceship Earth*, produced a positively space-age, low-weight car back in 1933. Known as the Dymaxion, it was streamlined, could cross open fields, accelerate to 120 mph, make a 180-degree turn in its own length, travel at 28 mpg and carry twelve passengers. Yet it was never marketed.

In fact, for the past two decades cars have been getting heavier: a trend probably more linked with the successful selling of weight-equals-safety than with the spreading girth of their unfit drivers. Unfortunately, heavier cars don't necessarily mean safer cars. (Never mind that the true definition of a safe car ought to be one that increases safety for all road users, not just the occupants of a lights-on, airbag-packed Volvo estate.) Indeed a Swedish insurance firm, Foksam, claims that the difference in crash resistance between a range of cars weighing about the same can be as high as 60 per cent.[3] These results aren't so surprising as a heavier, steel-framed car often has minimal weight directed towards safety features – whatever the ads may claim. The pounds pile on in relation to body size, engine volume and power.

'To accelerate the engine must be so big that it can use only a small fraction of its power for actual driving. For every five to seven gallons of fuel, only one gallon's worth of propulsion energy gets to the wheels of a car. The 15 to 20 per cent of fuel energy that does reach the wheels is used up in three ways: about a third gets lost accelerating and braking during city driving, another third in air friction, and the last third in heating the road and the tires. Of the energy delivered to the wheels, 95 per cent moves the car and only the remaining 5 per cent moves the drive. Thus only one per cent of the gasoline moves you to your destination,' claims the group working on the Hypercar at the Hypercar Center, part of the innovative Rocky Mountain Institute, which is based in glass offices in Western Colorado (but is so well insulated that bananas ripen even during the blizzard season).[4]

Two distinct problems need to be tackled: energy use during manufacture, and pollution escaping from car exhausts. The amount of energy used to manufacture the world's cars is huge and this adds to the problem of global warming. In the US around half the rubber, one-third of the platinum, one-sixth of the aluminium, one-seventh of the steel and one-tenth of the copper used is for car manufacture.[5] However, cutting back on manufacturing levels could mean job losses and a drop in the number of cars sold. Not surprisingly the motor industry has therefore looked to improvements in emission levels which help improve air quality – but it's come at a price for consumers. Between 1967 and 1990 the average US consumer has had to find 83 per cent more cash for their car.[6]

And, as author Michael Redclift points out, what is done is often too little, too late. 'Most environmental management is reactive, responding to pollution only when problems become very severe, or human health is involved . . . For example the pressure of acid rain leads to increased acidification of the environment and we respond, by putting catalytic converters on cars. These kinds of end-of-pipe measures are necessary, but not sufficient. . . . end-of-pipe "solutions" tend to be not only environmentally out-dated very quickly, but also extremely costly.'[7]

Don't blame us

The Society of Motor Manufacturers and Traders (SMMT) rejects charges that the manufacturers are failing to produce cleaner cars. SMMT is essentially the motor-trade lobby group. It has around a thousand members, including UK manufacturers like Honda, Rover, Nissan and Ford; traders who manufacture outside the UK such as Mercedes-Benz and

Volkswagen; component companies such as Lucas and GKN; as well as bus and lorry manufacturers. With such heavyweight backing it is little surprise that SMMT has a seat on the board of the British Roads Federation, which lobbies government to provide a modern, high-quality road network.

'The problem is that for over a century manufacturers have been developing new types of cars, from electric to fuel-cell, but, because the internal combustion engine is now so refined and very clean, it's difficult to improve on,' says David McConnell, government affairs manager. 'Now, and when the new regulations come into force from 2000 covering limit values of emissions, the internal combustion engine is by any definition low-emission. Many of the air-quality problems are the result of too many older vehicles on the roads.' Indeed, McConnell insists that it is now impossible to kill yourself by inhaling the exhaust from a new vehicle – though he admits the carbon monoxide might still give you a bad headache.

'If you are driving in a ten-year-old car the chances are that you are using leaded fuel and the car is a heavy polluter. So the manufacturers would encourage people to scrap these cars.' McConnell thinks the way to persuade people to upgrade to newer, cleaner models would be to follow the example of Denmark, France, Ireland and Italy where the government provides an incentive (around £500) to the car owner to replace it with a brand-new car. 'You can get a new car for seven to eight thousand pounds, not much more than the price of installing central heating,' says McConnell, 'and with government incentives the motor manufacturers could probably add similar incentives to win new business. That new car would then be able to do more than 150,000 low-emission miles if the motorist maintained the vehicle responsibly, which is a long time. People don't have to feel guilty, or that they are gross producers of emissions, providing they maintain their car and purchase as modern a car as possible.'

The only snag is that, although modernizing the twenty-five million or so cars on the UK's roads would improve air quality, especially in cities, it would have a *detrimental* effect on global warming because of the amount of energy which would need to be used to build the clean, new models. Currently the industry claims that cars contribute around 12 per cent towards UK man-made CO_2 – at the same time pointing out that the major sources of CO_2 are industry and power stations.[8] 'Not all motor manufacturers are convinced that they are contributing to climate change,' says McConnell, 'but for those concerned about CO_2 and energy use, you need to look at the whole life-cycle costs of the car. In terms of energy requirements a significant amount is used in production of the car itself. That's why some people think you should make cars which last longer, but there is a limit to how much retro fitting you can do. For example the old Citroën Dyane, so beloved of teachers, can only run on leaded petrol. But currently legislators seem more concerned with local air quality, so on balance scrapping and replacing vehicles with newer cars is the optimal solution.'

Alternative fuels are an obvious answer, but all fuels, from petrol to gas to electricity, have environmentally detrimental side effects. It's as if the engineers resist redesign that reflects the car's inspiration, the humble bike, a lesson enforced by the bitter experience of electronics genius Sir Clive Sinclair, who unveiled the £395 'C5' in January 1985. This lightweight, battery- and pedal-powered thirty-one-inch-high tricycle, with a range of twenty miles before recharging, was billed by Sir Clive as the answer to Britain's traffic problems. However, the C5 was launched during a cold snap, hardly the weather to encourage sceptical motoring correspondents to give up glamorous cars with solid roofs and centrally controlled heating. 'It cannot be regarded as serious, everyday, all-weather transport,' sneered one of its many critics.[9] Three months later production of the C5 was suspended. By October Sir Clive's company was in receivership, thanks to an idea before its time.

But authors Marsh and Collett think they know why the C5 was met with such derision: Sinclair foolishly let on that the C5 motor was just the same as the one used in a washing machine, and it was manufactured by Hoover. 'The real reason why the electric car is unable to find immediate acceptance is in the psychology of the car owner. Electric motors and internal combustion engines have quite different inherent symbolism. The former are associated primarily with domestic machinery, such as refrigerators and vacuum cleaners and home tools. It is not that they are women's motors – although they have a less than masculine image – it is the air of homely domesticity which makes them quite unacceptable as the motive force for a car.'[10] The C5 was speeded-up white goods, and there's nothing sexy about that.

Small cars

The Hypercar Center has dared to follow the Sinclair C5 by producing a small, neat machine. This hybrid invention has a scooter-sized engine. It is made of plug-in components which can be quickly replaced – even the engine can be assembled in just ten minutes. The result is a quiet, safe car (built of super-light carbon fibre, which absorbs crash energy better) which is around 95 per cent less polluting than a conventional car and manages a staggering 100–200 mpg. BMW has also fused the comfort of a car with the economy of a motorbike to produce the C1. A prototype was unveiled at the 1997 Frankfurt Motor

Show but isn't expected on the market until spring 2000.[11]

A similarly startling model was launched by Mercedes, at the same show, with its F300 Life-Jet. This is a three-wheeled, two-person machine which could be being used by commuters by 2001. First tests showed that one motor journalist thought it a hoot to drive as well as a 'serious attempt to bring the benefits of two and four-wheel vehicles together in a single machine'.[12] Certainly a much more generous conclusion than for the ill-fated Sinclair C5. Even so the story had a twist – the Dorset-based man, Cliff Ingram, who invented a very similar motorized tricycle, the Zero Lateral G, was forced to pull out of the race to create it because he could not afford the development, patent and assembly costs, totalling around £1,040,000. 'I feel very angry that I poured 5,000 hours of thought and development time into an idea I conceived 10 years ago – while enduring the prejudice shown towards inventors in this country only to be pipped at the post by Mercedes,' said Ingram.[13] Time and again ingenuity shown by environmental inventors has proved no match for cash backing.

In theory the Hypercar and vehicles like the C1 will be cheap, more in the scooter or bike price range than the car. And that has led society's dreamers to hope that it could be vehicles like these which help change the way we live. Instead of owning their own vehicles people will rent a vehicle on an as-needs basis – just like the bike- and car-share experiments in Copenhagen.

Power problems

If you count Britain's seventeen thousand milkfloats, then this country boasts the greatest number of electric vehicles in the world. But the truth is that there are still very few other vehicles using this power source, no more than two hundred in the UK, including fourteen doing trials in Coventry, three of which are being used by the Royal Mail. France has many more electric cars on the roads, nearly three thousand now that an electric Peugeot 106 model can be bought.

Director of the Electric Vehicle Association (EVA) Brian Roden believes there are some tough barriers to the success of electric vehicles, including their expense and lack of availability. 'An electric vehicle is ideal for the two-car family as the second car tends to be used for short journeys like child delivery, shopping or trips to the bridge club. Often they do less than five thousand miles a year, which is about twelve to fourteen miles a day, a range that the electric batteries can easily cope with. However, although vehicles are expensive to buy or convert, within four or five years you will get that back from savings on your running costs. This is a strong argument for individuals, but it isn't any more for councils, many of whom aren't able to budget five years ahead.'

The EVA believes the electric vehicle is an ideal short-term solution to environmental problems. 'It could make an impact now if people adopted it. At least 5 per cent of the vehicle population could be electric vehicles, particularly those used in urban situations for deliveries such as the local council's meals on wheels, the pool car used by planning inspectors, electricity boards and so on,' says Roden. Indeed, his ambition is to see at least 20 per cent of local-authority vehicles converted to electric power.

Environmental campaigners at Greenpeace have been working on electric runarounds, unveiling the electric-powered Smile back in 1996. This was an eco-friendly model based on the popular Continental family car the Renault Twingo, produced by three Swiss companies, with 43 per cent less fuel consumption than a conventional Twingo (or a Ford Escort or Volkswagen Polo). Its weight had been slashed by a quarter and its drag coefficient reduced.

Greenpeace Germany, which spent £1.1 million creating the cleaner car, is motivated by fears of global warming. And as a result it has done a better job, so far, than most of the world's car manufacturers, even though they promised to cut the fuel consumption of the average new car by 10 per cent between the early 1990s and 2005. But as cars have become heavier (up to 30 per cent between 1990 and 1996), fuel efficiency has stagnated. Not surprisingly Thilo Bode, executive director of Greenpeace International, views this as irresponsible: 'The car industry is obstructing feasible technology which would help prevent climate change.'[14] Brian Roden does too: 'Companies are doing research, but a lot of it is window-dressing. They can't afford to ignore the trends, so they put just enough into research to ensure that they won't get too far behind if something does take off.'

One of the first cars Mrs Henry Ford drove was electric-powered. Indeed, the first driver to die in Britain after a motor accident, Henry Lindfield on 12 February 1898, was also using an electric car.[15] Yet many people are hailing electric-powered cars as the new nirvana.

Battery power

Already there are several thousand battery-powered electric vehicles being driven around the world. General Motors unveiled the sporty-looking EV1 for use in California and Arizona at the end of 1996. But they are pricey – the EV1 sells for US$34,000, although it can be leased for $399 a month. Toyota's RAV4 EV, which looks like the company's sport-utility vehicles and has a range of two hundred kilometres per charge, can be leased for \$1,680 a month.[16] The only ready-for-the-road production models available in Britain are the Peugeot 106 and Citroën Saxo.

Fuel cells

The first fuel cell was invented in the 1830s by William Grove. Modern fuel cells generate power from hydrogen and oxygen, creating electricity without the need for combustion, so that the only emissions are electricity, heat and water. However, fuel cells were not looked at with much attention until World War II. Since then fuel-cell use is best known in the space programme.

The advantage of a fuel cell for powering cars is that it can produce electrical energy for a much longer time than a battery. Working with fuel-cell pioneers from the Canadian outfit Ballard Power Systems, the German company Mercedes-Benz looks set to be the first to market a fuel-cell-powered A-class Mercedes in 2004. Already Ford has a £600 million project to mass-produce fuel-cell vehicles by 2006.[17] General Motors and Toyota also look set to be in competition.

What next?

Until solar (or even wind) power is further developed it looks as if fuel cells may well be the best way forward for electric vehicles. Los Angeles automotive market analyst Chris Cedergren claims: 'I think the battery electric vehicle is not a viable alternative for 20–25 years. The only way it will work is if it offers the same performance and practicality at the same price as continental cars. People have got less and less time for their activities and want more and more convenience, which the battery vehicle does not provide.'[18]

Despite this there are trials by Audi, BMW, Chrysler, Citroën, Daewoo, Fiat, Honda, Kia, Mazda, Reliant, Rover, Toyota,

Vauxhall's parent General Motors, Volkswagen and Volvo.[19] Are they going down the wrong road? As Ford points out: 'Fuel cells have three key advantages over batteries for electric vehicles. They will cost less, they don't have the range limitations of batteries and their durability is not limited.'[20]

Yet Brian Roden from the EVA insists that the battery electric vehicle is a better short-term answer. 'Perhaps the long-term future is with the fuel cell. But it's at least five years away from commercial availability and even that may prove to be optimistic. People can and should buy electric-battery vehicles now to do their limited-range jobs. If we all wait for the fuel cell to come it may never arrive.'

Sun power

One alternative to electricity is solar power. The F1 car of the solar world is Honda's concept car, the Dream, which won the 1996 World Solar Challenge, hitting speeds of 90kmh over three thousand kilometres of Australian desert. But, at £856,000, it is not likely to be the way we get around in the future.[21] However, its spin-off, the Honda ZLEV (zero-level-emission vehicle) engine, appearing in the Honda Accord in 1998, claims it cuts pollution to one-thousandth of the levels produced by a conventional petrol engine – making its exhaust cleaner than the air around the car in cities like Tokyo, Los Angeles and Bangkok.[22]

Biofuel

Biofuels are power sources produced by transforming certain crops, like alcohol-distilled sugar cane, into ethanol. Biofuels have been used to power an increasing number of Brazilian vehicles since 1975 in a bid to deal with the oil shocks of the 1970s. However, many environmentalists point out that it makes no sense growing crops to power vehicles when there is a shortfall of fertile agricultural land in so many countries. For example an average Brazilian distillery producing 180,000

Buffalo stance to polluting tour

Pop singer Neneh Cherry's 1998 world tour will satisfy one set of auditors – the carbon number crunchers. After Dr Richard Tipper at Edinburgh University worked out that the pollution resulting from her tour – from road transport, flights, electricity used at the gigs and hotels, as well as her fans travelling to the gigs – would be two thousand tons of CO_2, Neneh decided to do some carbon-offsetting. To make up for the massive dose of CO_2 the tour's producing, Neneh will plant 2500 trees around the UK. As Tipper reckons five trees soak up four tons of CO_2, this should reset the balance, even if some of the new trees die.

Neneh may have had the first environment-friendly tour, but the carbon-audit scheme is also gaining momentum with other groups, including Formula 1, advertising agency J. Walter Thompson, Whole Earth Foods, Gorgeous Films, Imagination Design Group and the Levellers. Many of the bands playing at Glastonbury contribute to carbon-offsetting by planting trees in the Glastonbury Festival forest.

The carbon-audit scheme has been developed by Daniel Morrell through his organization Future Forests (01963 350465) litres a day requires eleven thousand hectares of land for sugar-cane production and produces thirteen litres of stillage waste for every litre of alcohol produced. Already Brazilian distilleries cultivate more than fifty-five thousand hectares, but few countries have so much space available.[23]

Gas

Gas conversions seem to be all the rage at Westminster. John Major had his car converted, and now Blair is embarking on dual gas/petrol conversions of his government's vehicles, including his own family's people mover. Volvo also produces a model which runs on compressed natural gas and petrol, and doesn't cost more than a petrol-powered vehicle. So, this might be the way to go – if only there were more than eighteen gas stations around the country.

There are a number of alternative gas fuels currently being used by drivers. Already a million vehicles use natural gas (either compressed natural gas, known as CNG, or liquefied natural gas, LNG) and another four million vehicles use liquefied petroleum gas (also known as LPG or propane). Organizations like the Energy Saving Trust, which is helping to promote the use of these gases as an alternative to petrol and diesel, to enable Britain to reduce its CO_2 emissions in a bid to reduce global warming, are particularly targeting fleet managers rather than private drivers.

But the main hiccup with a number of the new power sources – fuel-cell, electric and gas – is that there is almost no infrastructure suitable for the public to use for refuelling or recharging in the way that petrol stations are so accessible. For example, in Japan there are just forty-six recharging points for electric cars – with just two in Tokyo available for the public.[24]

'Already motor manufacturers can supply some of these vehicles,' says David McConnell of the SMMT, 'but it requires someone to invest in an infrastructure drive which supports the drivers – and that's not the responsibility of manufacturers.' Unless the oil companies undergo a major shift in business interests they are unlikely to provide this vital support. As a result expect to see short-term solutions in the form of hybrid cars which are able to switch between two different power systems – at high speeds petrol can be used, and in town, the electric battery. It's a solution which looks set to satisfy initial environmental demands, with the practicality of keeping the car on the road. However, even these new cars are not pollution-free, because fossil fuels tend to be used to generate the electricity and hydrogen to run their engines – which means more global warming at the extraction or power-station stage.

Conceptual spin

This is where concept cars come in. These are the space-age vehicles wheeled out for motor shows by manufacturers. Some people think of these displays as modern freak shows – and certainly the guffaws from people seeing Renault's Zoom, an electric car which could shorten its wheelbase by folding up its back end to suit the cramped parking spaces of Paris, at the 1997 Earls Court Motor Show suggested the public wouldn't be buying this model, even though it boasts 95 mpg. However, the car still secured plenty of media coverage.

'Concept cars at the motor shows are not just there for PR reasons, they are a practical display of the technology for journalists and potential customers to look at. But many do make their way on to the road, it's just that few are a commercial success,' says David McConnell.

There's a good reason for that, admits Renault, which is one of the companies with a reputation of working up its designs ready for public sale. 'A lot of concept cars are created with a million-pound budget,' says press officer Richard Hammond; 'so though they may look innovative they are too expensive to end up on the road. There is another catch: designers often want to show their new ideas to gauge the response, but it may take a while for mainstream technology to catch up.'

The public seems to have made faster progress with transforming the traditional car shape. At the hot-rod track over-accessorized Ford Cortinas are *de rigueur* – especially Batmobiles.[25] Recently a builder's skip, with a Mini chassis and a top speed of 80 mph, made a mockery of jibes about the open-top Lada being nothing more than a stationary skip when it skipped to victory in a bizarre vehicle chase organized by the *Sun* newspaper at Donnington Park circuit in Leicestershire. Challengers included Britain's fastest shed, a souped-up armchair and a speedboat.[26]

George Shields from Melbourne, Derbyshire, who converted the second-placed garden shed into a 55 mph 'car', claimed it was easy to make. 'I just had to extend it to get the quad bike to fit inside,' said the farmer, who built it to take a bridegroom friend to his wedding.[27] The DoT rules that all vehicles on the road must have a numberplate, so when my dad's life-sized mechanical elephant, Jessica, which he rented out for kids' rides, was on the road a numberplate had to be tied to her tail.

New generation

Why, after one hundred years of self-satisfied replication, are manufacturers suddenly pouring money into a new generation of models? Is this new sensitivity brought on by the world

---

Bottle bank

Increasingly cars will be made of material that has been recycled, rather than materials which *could* be recycled. Examples of the latter include Renault's Mégane Scenic, which boasts that 60 per cent of the car's plastic content could be recycled, or the newer Saabs, which are 95 per cent recyclable. But such claims suggest that manufacturers aren't playing the 'reuse' card straight: all cars have recyclable parts, as junk dealers and fans of the autojumble are well aware.

However, Chrysler has devised an economical (50 mpg in town) and cheap (£4000) car which is made of 2132 two-litre recycled plastic drinks bottles mixed with glass-fibre reinforcing material. Known as the Composite Concept Vehicle (CCV), it is modelled on the Citroën 2CV and is designed for use in developing countries, to fill the gap between scooters and imported Western cars. Not only does the CCV take less time to build than conventional cars (just over six hours compared to eighteen hours for other small Chrysler cars like the Neon saloon), its design makes it almost 100 per cent recyclable.[28]

---

entering the Aquarian Age, by the millennium or by something more hard-nosed? The answer is straightforward. It's not just that there are too many cars on the roads; there is also a world-wide glut of cars. 'If all the car firms in the world ran flat out, they could produce 68,000,000 cars a year. In 1996, they actually made 50,000,000 – 73 per cent of capacity. It is worse in some places than others. In Western Europe, car makers turn out around 6,000,000 fewer vehicles than they could; in Japan

4,000,000 fewer and 3,900,000 fewer in North America. For the firms this is bad news. Car companies are accustomed to making their really big bucks when operating at over 80 per cent capacity.'[29]

It's not too cynical to say that Greener cars equal a marketable new product. And the over-production glut is speeding up that process. As General Motors' head of research Ken Baker (who was behind the EV1's development) puts it: 'Right now, environmental questions are an issue for society rather than the market. But the environment will be an issue of competitiveness in five to ten years. It seems wise to be there before it happens, with products in place.'[30]

It's not just electric windows any more, or an automated voice telling you to 'Belt up' or that 'The door is open' – these days there are even self-driving cars. Disney's invention Herbie was fantasy, but Mitsubishi's HSR-VI, launched at the 1997 Frankfurt Motor Show, could herald the age when cars know they are a 'somebody'.[31] This model will switch between manual drive for built-up areas and automated driving on main roads. It's all controlled by an on-board computer which provides the driver with information about traffic conditions from laser units, stereo-image cameras and roadside multi-communication systems. In theory cars could exchange information between themselves. A time may come when you can take your hands off the wheel and get on with your life: catch up on paperwork, read, use the mobile, perhaps even have a beer. Controlling cars in fleets of ten or twelve vehicles has already been tested on a San Diego highway.

There's just one snag to this driverless car business: it's rather *déjà vu*. After all, isn't that old-fashioned beast, the train or the bus, a type of driverless car?

CHAPTER ELEVEN

The estate we're in

Predicting the end of the car's hold on our culture is a risky business. It seems that the car, together with its most avid supporters, has inveigled us into believing that we can't live our lives, or even have the quality of life we expect, without instant access to a motor. Driving seems to be the most adult thing any of us ever does – and, as columnist Suzanne Moore put it after revealing that her New Year's resolution was to learn to drive aged thirty-seven, it couldn't be that hard because: 'If every other moron could drive, then so could I.'[1] Sadly she's right: as a result those people without a licence, a car, or the latest model may find themselves driving against the tide of what's considered normal behaviour. But the fact is that we have to change our ways, now.

Unless individuals opt for more sustainable ways of travelling, taking to the road in your own car is likely to get a great deal more expensive, through the imposition of more tolls and higher taxes. It's a point many drivers already understand, claim a number of MPs, including the junior minister responsible for transport in London, Glenda Jackson. 'People now accept we can't go on the way we are. There have to be alternatives to the way we move ourselves and goods around,' she said on the radio programme *Desert Island Discs* recently.

Journalist Bryan Appleyard makes the same point: 'Motoring, in the old sense, was a great and wonderful thing. Driving a great car remains one of the finest 20th century experiences. But, like so many other fine experiences, it is not something that can be had every day. If motoring is to live, the car, as we currently know it, must die.'[2]

But, like reports of Mark Twain's death, the demise of the car has been exaggerated. After all, in 1958 author John Keats wrote a diatribe against post-war auto culture in the US: 'The American's marriage to the American automobile is now at an end, and it is only a matter of minutes to the final pistol shot, although who pulls the trigger has yet to be determined.'[3]

Well, it hasn't happened yet. So we might as well face it: while there's oil to be squeezed out of the planet we'll never walk the roads alone. And in oil-producing countries where fuel is kept so cheap – cheaper than Coca-Cola even – it is unlikely that any efforts will be made towards fuel economy in the near future. It's even been claimed that 'Cheap gasoline for ever, whatever' is an unwritten part of the American Constitution. Nevertheless the post-petrol age is coming soon and that may finally trigger a massive change in our single-minded pursuit of a set of car keys and an off-street parking place.

Until then there is a lot that could be done to try to ensure that car drivers stop bullying people who either don't have, or don't so readily use, their own vehicle. And that requires drivers and non-drivers to take more responsibility for the way they get around. The obvious change we can all make is to work out if we really need to use our car for every journey. Using the car less may be the first step to changing ingrained driving habits. It may also turn out to be a way of getting fitter, if you decide to walk or cycle to the postbox or corner shop rather than always driving there.

There are also many proactive ways to speed up the change to a more sustainable transport strategy. You could become a member of the well-respected lobby group Transport 2000; contribute to Local Agenda 21 initiatives in the county or city where you live; donate to RoadPeace's work; or invite someone from a campaign group to speak at your parish council, local community centre or social club. You could join local groups like FoE and CPRE to fight unsustainable developments like new roads at the public inquiry stage, or join protesters at their camps and street demonstrations.

On the holiday front you can opt for places where you don't need a car. For example you could go to Cornwall or Devon by train, which gives you the added benefit of avoiding the bank-holiday jams. You could ring groups like the National Trust to find out which of their properties can be visited using public transport. Or you could try using the cycle routes criss-crossing the country, adapted by cycling organization Sustrans primarily for cyclists, walkers and the disabled.

It may be possible to team up with a like-minded friend or friends and develop a car-sharing strategy. Many people already do this through the school run. But what about shopping trips – is there a neighbour who would benefit, and contribute towards the petrol at the same time? You may even find it more convenient to take the bus to town, avoiding the multi-storey car-parking queues, and a taxi back.

Perhaps you could switch your car insurance and car-recovery policy to a group that will not lobby for new roads, like the Environmental Transport Association.

And if you're a parent you could work out what really worries you about letting your kids get to school on their own. Is it a particular road crossing? Is it the speed cars go beside the pavements your children must use? Is it because the headteacher won't let them park bikes inside the school grounds? Perhaps there are no cycle lanes? If one of these is a problem, then work with other parents to lobby the council or school for changes. You could even set up a rota to help escort younger kids to the school.

Some people may find that reading this book brings on guilt pangs when they drive to the recycling centre or treat the kids at that new drive-in McDonald's. But the message many Greens want to get across is that you don't have to wait for other people to do the changing – you can do it yourself, especially as most car journeys are so short. Even if your small change of behaviour seems insignificant, it isn't. After all, if you're not part of the solution you can be certain you are part of the problem.

Useful Contacts

Accident support

Brake, PO Box 272, Dorking, Surrey RH4 4FR (01306 741113). A road-safety organization which works to stop death, injury and trauma on the roads. Brake's booklet, *Coping With Grief When Someone You Love is Killed on the Roads*, is distributed to bereaved people by police, hospitals and counselling services.

RoadPeace, PO Box 2579, London NW10 3PW (0181 964 9353). Influential national charity for road-traffic victims, including a helpline for relatives and victims: 0181 964 1021.

Alternative power

Electric Vehicle Association, Alexandra House, Harrowden Road, Wellingborough, Northants NN8 5BD (01933 276618). Contact EVA for information about where to buy an EV or convert your vehicle to run on electric power.

Energy Saving Trust, 11-12 Buckingham Gate, London SW1E 6LB (0345 277200). The government- and private-funded organization has a three-year programme, ending in

1999, which offers grants to fleet managers for half of the additional cost needed to buy a dedicated or converted alternative vehicle. Currently for large electric vehicles this can be up to £5000; for LPG £1500 and for CNG £2000–£2500.

Better driving

Institute of Advanced Motorists, IAM House, 359 Chiswick High Road, London W4 4HS (0181 994 4403). Contact the IAM for information about their two hundred local groups, skill-building and the ninety-minute advanced driving test (for both car drivers and motor-cyclists). It is recommended that you read the official manual *Pass Your Advanced Driving Test* or *Pass Your Advanced Motorcycling Test*, both £7.99. Phone orders may be taken on the IAM number or by fax: 0181 994 9249.

Pass Plus Board, c/o Association of British Insurers, 51 Gresham Street, London EC2V 7HQ (0171 600 3333). The Pass Plus scheme, run by the Department of Transport, the Driving Standards Agency and the Association of British Insurers, aims to encourage newly qualified drivers to be safer and better drivers on the roads. It consists of a course of six training sessions designed as a follow-on from the driving test. Pass Plus holders may be eligible for lower insurance rates.

Royal Society for the Prevention of Accidents, Edgbaston Park, 353 Bristol Road, Birmingham B5 7ST (0121 248 2000). Drivers who pass their one-and-a-quarter-hour-long test will still be expected to take a refresher test at three-year intervals. It is recommended that you read the police driver's handbook, *Roadcraft*, available from bookshops. Other tests include defensive driving, in-vehicle training for company-car drivers and a national minibus test.

Breakdown, road patrol and/or traffic advice services

AA (0800 444999) The Automobile Association has more than nine million members. It runs patrols, arranges insurance and hotel bookings and broadcasts traffic bulletins, and is working on new information technology for improved services. Members also receive a quarterly magazine.

The Environmental Transport Association, 10 Church Street, Weybridge, Surrey KT13 8RS (01932 828882). Provides a breakdown service and co-ordinates the annual Green Transport Week and National Car-Free Day, both in June. For more information, ideas, education and action packs see its website at: http://www.eta.co.uk

RAC (0800 029029). Ranks alongside the AA as the breakdown-recovery giant. It provides vehicle users with a range of breakdown-recovery services whether you are a driver or passenger. For more information also see the website: http://www.rac.co.uk

Campaign groups

Alarm UK (0181 983 3572). An alliance against damaging road schemes. Most of the UK's anti-roads groups are part of Alarm UK.

The Council for the Protection of Rural England (0171 976 6433). Active locally, nationally and internationally working for a beautiful and living countryside. CPRE specializes in some transport-related work, such as effects on the countryside, planning and energy use.

Friends of the Earth (0171 490 1555). FoE campaigns on a range of environmental issues nationally and internationally, including transport. There are local groups nationwide.

Greenpeace (0171 865 8100). Uses non-violent direct action to highlight its environmental campaigns. One of its key focuses at the moment is climate change and energy use.

Reclaim the Streets, PO Box 9656, London N4 4JY. Uses non-violent direct action to protest against cars and traffic at the same time as offering a vision of what excellent places streets could be without traffic. Try its website: http://www.hrc.wmin.ac/uk/campaigns/rts.html

Transport 2000, Walkden House, 10 Melton Street, London NW1 2EJ (0171 388 8386). A national and environmental transport campaign which is aiming to produce integrated and environmentally safer public transport. Specific campaigns include Home Zones and Streets for People. Transport 2000 is a membership organization which also produces an excellent, lively magazine, *Transport Retort*.

Car shares

European Car Sharing (contact Joachim Schwarz in Bremen, fax: 00 49 421 74465). ECS is an umbrella group offering consultancy services for groups interested in the city car club concept. It was formed in 1991 and has more than forty members which operate shared cars for around twenty thousand people in 250 towns in Germany, Austria, Switzerland and the Netherlands.

Cycling promotion and cycle parking

Bikepark Covent Garden, 14 Stukeley Street, London WC2 (0171 430 0083).

Bikepark King's Road, The Courtyard, 250 King's Road, London SW3 6NT (0171 565 0778).

Cyclists' Touring Club, 69 Meadrow, Godalming, Surrey GU7 3HS (01483 417217). CTC is Britain's largest national cycling organization, with around forty thousand individual members, more than two hundred local groups and a further two hundred affiliated clubs. It co-ordinates National Bike Week in June.

Sustrans (0117 929 0888). Designs and builds traffic-free routes for cyclists, walkers and the disabled. By early 1998, 1400 of the total 6500 miles of the National Cycle Route Network had been completed, including the West Country Way (Padstow to Bristol and Bath); a coast-to-coast route across the Pennines; Inverness to Carlisle, the east coast between Hull and Harwich; and a section in Wales from Holyhead to Cardiff and on to Chepstow. During 1998 stretches between the Clyde and the Forth, and Hull to Middlesbrough, are due to be opened. Sustrans is also working with local authorities to devise safe routes to school.

Holidays and day trips without cars

Association of National Parks (01647 440245). The ANP recommends ringing the park you wish to visit for details about how it can be reached by public transport and any restrictions on private-vehicle access:

Brecon Beacons (01874 624437); Broads Authority (01603 310734); Dartmoor (01626 832093); Exmoor (01398 323665); Lake District (01539 724555); New Forest (01703 284144); North York Moors (01439 770657); Northumberland (01434 605555); Peak District (01629 816200); Pembrokeshire (01437 764636); Snowdonia (01766 770274); Yorkshire Dales (01969 650456).

National Trust (0181 315 1111). A handful of NT properties can *only* be reached by public transport, such as Prior Park in Bath. For information about how to reach NT properties by public transport use the annual *National Trust Handbook* or call its information service.

North York Moors Historical Railway Trust, Pickering Station, Pickering, North Yorkshire YO18 7AJ (talking timetable: 01751 473535). Website: http://www.nymr. demon.co.uk

Other ideas

1) Contact the nearest tourist office for information about public transport.
2) Consider using taxis or a hired car.

Professional groups

Car Free Cities Network, c/o 18 Square de Meeus, B-1050, Brussels, Belgium (fax: 00 32 2 552 0889). A group of sixty or more European cities attempting to confront the conflicting demands between road traffic and the human right to health, as described in its Copenhagen Declaration of Mobility. It produces an inspiring magazine, *Car Free Cities*.

Road Danger Reduction Forum, PO Box 2944, London NW10 2AX. Brings together professionals to discuss topical issues and has some useful publications, including an occasional newsletter, *New Agenda*.

Public transport

National Express. For bus timetable information and credit-card booking, 8am–10pm (0990 808080).

Oxford Tube (01865 772250). Twenty-four-hour information hotline about its twenty-four-hour bus services between Oxford and London. Details can also be found at http://www. oxlink.co.uk/oxford/tube/

Train timetable information for all services (0345 484950). You will be given the phone number for the relevant company to make an advance credit-card booking. Ask about apex tickets, super savers, savers and off-peak travel times, or any other discount scheme, to ensure you can obtain your ticket for less than the full commuter fare.

Other ideas

For local bus timetables try contacting your council which may have a dedicated travel information line about public transport services, like Hertfordshire's.

Shopping without cars

Iceland offers free same-day home delivery for anyone spending £25 or over. There is also a home shopping (catalogue-style) service. Ask at your local store or contact general enquiries (0500 876553).

Sainsbury's has a growing range of remote shopping services. For details see the website: http://www.sainsburys.co.uk

Tesco runs a home shopper service for those with Internet facilities. You need Microsoft Internet Explorer 3 to access Internet Superstore for on-line browsing and ordering. There is also a CD-ROM, Tesco Home Shopper, which you can use to send orders via the Internet. Tesco Direct is on http://www.tesco.co.uk; for home shopping call 0345 225533 or fax 0138 2819956. There is also a gift-collection and baby-catalogue service.

Traidcraft (0191 491 0855) Catalogue service of fairly traded gifts and foods (including muesli, jams, dried fruit, coffee and tea) with door-to-door delivery.

Other ideas

1) Ask local shops if they can deliver goods to your door.
2) Try buying vegetables from a locally organized 'vegetable box' scheme. Some schemes deliver, some provide a nearby drop-off point. Contact the **Soil Association**, Bristol House, Victoria Street, Bristol BS1 6DF (01179 290661) for information about box schemes. See also *Where to Buy Organic Food*, £4.50.

Video news

Undercurrents, 16b Cherwell Street, Oxford OX4 1BG (01865 203661; credit-card orders accepted on 01865 203662 or fax 01865 243562). Produces regular alternative news on a seventy-minute video. It also offers campaigners camcorder training. Director Thomas Harding has written a handbook for camcorder campaigners, *The Video Activist Handbook* (Pluto Press, 1997, ISBN 0 745 31169 5), £11.99. Undercurrents' website is: http://www.undercurrents.org

Walking groups

The Pedestrians Association, 126 Aldersgate Street, London EC1A 4JQ (0171 490 0750). The organization campaigns to improve conditions for walking both nationally and through its local branches. Walk to School Week is co-ordinated by the Pedestrians Association.

The Ramblers Association, 1–5 Wandsworth Road, London SW8 2XY (0171 582 6878). Campaigns for walkers' rights and produces a regular magazine.

Notes

Chapter One: Cars R us

1. Emrys Jones, *Metropolis: The World's Great Cities*, Oxford: Oxford University Press, 1990.
2. *Evening Standard*, 18 February 1997.
3. *Sunday Times*, 8 June 1997.
4. *Squall*, Autumn 1995.
5. John Adams, Professor of Geography at the University of London, Fuming Mad Rally, London, 27 September 1997. He is using a standard parking space of twenty feet.
6. *Observer*, 30 November 1997.
7. *Auto-Free Times*, Summer 1997.
8. *Environment Digest*, issue 4/5, 1997.
9. West Ham v. Huddersfield programme, 29 September 1997; West Ham v. Liverpool programme, 27 September 1997.
10. Desmond Morris, *The Human Zoo*, London: Corgi, 1969.
11. *Guardian*, 29 April 1997.
12. *Guardian*, 12 May 1997.

13. See also Kerry Hamilton, Linda Jenkins, Abigail Gregory, *Women and Transport: Bus Deregulation in West Yorkshire*, University of Bradford, 1991.

14. Retail Motor Industry Federation Ltd (RMI), *Facts Not Fiction*, 1997.

15. *Sun*, 19 September 1997.

16. Jonathan Wood, *Wheels of Misfortune*, London: Sidgwick & Jackson, 1988.

17. Ibid.

18. Mark Liniado, *Car Culture and Countryside Change*, Cirencester: National Trust, 1996.

19. *Independent*, 18 January 1996.

20. Cited at Local Agenda 21 meeting, Islington, 14 April 1997.

Chapter Two: Car culture

1. *Daily Telegraph*, 1 March 1997.

2. Royal Mail, Press Release with first day cover, 1 October 1996.

3. John Butman, *Car Wars*, London: Grafton, 1991.

4. *Evening Standard*, 22 April 1997.

5. *Sunday Times*, 28 September 1997.

6. Peter Marsh, Peter Collett, *Driving Passion: The Psychology of the Car*, London: Jonathan Cape, 1986.

7. *Daily Telegraph*, 22 November 1997.

8. Barry Norman, *The Film Greats*, London: Hodder & Stoughton, 1985.

9. *Telegraph Magazine*, 31 May 1997.

10. Kenneth Grahame, *The Wind in the Willows*, London: Methuen & Co, 1970.

11. Will Self, 'Scale', in *Grey Area*, London: Bloomsbury, 1994.

12.	Heathcote Williams, *Autogeddon*, London: Jonathan Cape, 1991.

13.	Ben Elton, *Gridlock*, London: Warner, 1991.

Chapter Three: Dead time

1.	The Henley Centre, *Media Futures 1997*, 1997.

2.	Ibid.

3.	*Le Sauvage*, September–October 1973.

4.	*Sunday Times*, 1 February 1997.

5.	*Guardian*, 30 June 1997.

6.	*Leicester Spokes*, no. 48, Autumn 1997.

7.	*Evening Standard*, 29 May 1997.

8.	Ibid.

9.	Transport 2000, *Changing Journeys to Work*, 1997.

10.	*Transport Retort*, no. 19, July/August 1996.

11.	*The Times*, 6 December 1997.

12.	*Economist*, 25 November 1996.

13.	*Evening Standard*, 20 June 1997.

14.	*Islington Society Newsletter*, October 1997.

15.	*Green Futures*, October/November 1997.

16.	*Guardian*, 26 September 1997.

17.	*New Statesman*, 21 November 1997.

18.	*Green Futures*, October/November 1997.

19.	*Economist*, 22 June 1996.

20.	LA21 initiatives have been started by more than two thousand local authorities in fifty-one countries, according to *The Way Forward: Beyond Agenda 21*, ed. Felix Dodds, London: Earthscan, 1997.

21.	*Economist*, 19 July 1997.

22.	Harley Sherlock, *Cities Are Good for Us*, London: Paladin, 1991, available from Transport 2000.

23.	Steering Group on the study of the long-term problems

of traffic in towns: *Traffic in Towns: A Study of the Long-term Problems of Traffic in Urban Areas*, London: HMSO, 1963.

24. *Do or Die: Voices from Earth First!*, no. 5, 1996.
25. *Sunday Times*, 1 February 1997.
26. *Sunday Telegraph*, 5 August 1997.

Chapter Four: Open road

1. Harold Perkin, *The Age of the Automobile*, London: Quartet, 1976.
2. Roland Smith, *On Foot in the Yorkshire Dales*, Newton Abbot: David & Charles, 1996.
3. Clough Williams-Ellis, *England and the Octopus*, London: Bles, 1928.
4. *Guardian*, 8 August 1997.
5. *Earthmatters*, Summer 1996.
6. Statutory Tourist Boards of the UK, *The UK Tourist Statistics 1996*, July 1997.
7. *Evening Standard*, 29 May 1997.
8. Herbert Girardet, *The Gaia Atlas of Cities: New Directions for Sustainable Urban Living*, London: Gaia Books, 1996.
9. *Essex Protector*, n.d.
10. *Economist*, 22 June 1996.
11. The Henley Centre, *Media Futures 1997*.
12. *Autocar*, 15 October 1997.
13. *Times Magazine*, 15 November 1997.

Chapter Five: Fatal attraction

1. Perkin, *The Age of the Automobile*.
2. Winfried Wolf, *The Car Society*, London: Pluto, 1997.
3. Ibid.

4. Department of Transport Road Accident Unit.

5. *Big Issue*, 22 September 1997.

6. *Independent*, 28 November 1997.

7. *Guardian*, 28 July 1997.

8. *Guardian*, 24 September 1997.

9. *Independent on Sunday*, 17 August 1997.

10. Department of Transport.

11. *Guardian*, 27 October 1997.

12. *Independent on Sunday*, 21 January 1996.

13. Ralph Nader, *Unsafe at Any Speed: The Designed-in Dangers of the American Automobile*, New York: Grossman Bantam, 1965.

14. Marsh and Collett, *Driving Passion*.

15. Frances Basham, Bob Ughatti, *Car Culture*, London: Plexus, 1984.

16. Lex Service PLC, *Lex Report on Motoring*, 22 January 1997.

17. *Evening Standard*, 27 January 1997.

18. *Brakenews*, Autumn 1997.

19. Niki Lauda, *To Hell and Back: An Autobiography*, London: Stanley Paul, 1985.

20. *Guardian*, 6 September 1995.

21. *New Times*, 14 September 1996.

22. *Evening Standard*, 15 May 1996.

23. *Evening Standard*, 20 March 1997.

24. *Guardian*, 6 September 1995.

25. *Guardian*, 24 November 1997.

26. *Evening Standard*, 27 June 1997.

27. *Sunday Times*, 27 July 1997.

28. *Auto Express*, 24 September 1997.

29. Russell Lewis, *Margaret Thatcher: A Personal and Political Biography*, London: Routledge & Kegan Paul, 1984.

30. Ludovic Kennedy, *On my Way to the Club: The Autobiography of Ludovic Kennedy*, London: Collins, 1989.

31. P. J. O'Rourke, *Holidays in Hell*, London: Picador, 1989.

32. Nader, *Unsafe at Any Speed*.

33. Ibid.

34. Tim Beaumont, *The End of the Yellowbrick Road*, Charlbury, Oxon: John Carpenter, 1997.

35. London Borough of Islington, *Road Safety Plan 1996–2000*, 22 May 1996.

36. *Guardian*, 27 September 1997.

37. *Sun*, 11 December 1997.

38. *Mirror*, 26 September 1997.

39. *F1 Racing*, February 1997.

40. *Guardian*, 2 June 1997.

41. *Telegraph Magazine*, 4 October 1997.

42. *Hello!*, 20 September 1997.

43. *Guardian*, 27 November 1997.

44. Graham Coster, *A Thousand Miles from Nowhere: Trucking Two Continents*, London: Viking, 1995.

45. *Animal People; Kangaroo: A Road Movie*, BBC1, 1 October 1997.

46. *Daily Telegraph*, 22 November 1997.

47. *Daily Star*, 21 August 1997.

48. *Sun*, 30 August 1997.

49. Lex Service plc, *Driving for Safety 1997*.

50. Ibid.

51. *Evening Standard*, 20 September 1996.

52. *Auto Express*, 24 September 1997.

53. Based on *Time Out*, 10–17 September 1997.

Chapter Six: Protest and survive

1. *Guardian*, 2 October 1997.
2. *Economist*, 1 April 1995.
3. *The Times*, 24 November 1997.
4. John Whitelegg, *Critical Mass*, London: Pluto, 1997.
5. *The Times*, 24 November 1997.
6. Richard Rogers, *Cities for a Small Planet*, London: Faber & Faber, 1997.
7. Standing Advisory Committee on Trunk Road Assessment, *Trunk Roads and the Generation of Traffic*, 1994.
8. Barbara Bryant, *Twyford Down, Roads, Campaigning and Environmental Law*, London: E. & F. N. Spon, 1993.
9. *Salisbury Journal*, 27 February 1997.
10. CPRE files.
11. *Daily Mail*, 2 May 1995.
12. *Guardian*, 7 February 1996.
13. Mick Hamer, *Wheels Within Wheels*, London: Routledge & Kegan Paul, 1987.
14. *Earthmatters*, no. 30, Summer 1996.
15. *Management Today*, June 1996.
16. Barbara Bryant, *Twyford Down*.
17. *Ecologist*, vol. 23, no. 4, July/August 1996.
18. *Daily Telegraph*, 9 February 1996.
19. *BBC Wildlife* magazine, November 1996.
20. *Daily Telegraph*, 27, 31 January 1997, 3 June 1997.
21. *Loaded*, March 1996.
22. *Guardian*, 19 August 1996.
23. *Brighton Evening Argus*, 8 August 1997.

24.   *Evening Standard*, 26 November 1997.

25.   *Observer*, 30 November 1997.

26.   Whitelegg, *Critical Mass*.

Chapter Seven: Advertising gridlock

1.   *Time Out*, 26 March 1997.

2.   *Daily Telegraph*, 23 August 1997.

3.   David Ogilvy, *Ogilvy on Advertising*, London: Pan, 1983.

4.   *Campaign*, 10 May 1996.

5.   Gillian Dyer, *Advertising as Communication*, London: Routledge, 1988.

6.   ACNielsen.MEAL.

7.   Ogilvy, *Ogilvy on Advertising*.

8.   *Campaign*, 18 July 1997.

9.   Marsh and Collett, *Driving Passion*.

10.   *Guardian*, 11 March 1997.

11.   John Keats, *The Insolent Chariots*, Greenwich, Connecticut: C. Fawcett Publications, 1959.

12.   Marsh and Collett, *Driving Passion*.

13.   *The Times*, 20 June 1996.

14.   Whitelegg, *Critical Mass*.

15.   *Guardian*, 23 July 1997.

16.   *Guardian*, 16 July 1997.

17.   Ivan Illich, *Energy and Equity*, New York: Harper & Row, 1974.

18.   André Gorz, *Ecology as Politics*, London: Pluto, 1980.

19.   Ibid.

20.   *Independent*, 12 July 1997.

Chapter Eight: Get moving

1. Rogers, *Cities for a Small Planet*.
2. *Sunday Telegraph*, 8 June 1997.
3. Whitelegg, *Critical Mass*.
4. Children's Play Council, *Home Zones: Reclaiming Residential Streets*, 1997.
5. *Yorkshire Evening Press*, 25 September 1997.
6. City of York Council.
7. *The Times*, 8 June 1996.
8. *Permaculture*, no. 12, 1996.
9. *Green Futures*, June/July 1997.
10. *Independent on Sunday*, 21 January 1996.
11. Paul Brown, *Global Warming*, London: Blandford, 1996.
12. MORI, *Urban Environment*, 2 October 1997.
13. *New Scientist*, 24 January 1998.
14. *Guardian*, 21 August 1996.
15. *New Scientist*, 6 January 1996.
16. *Leicester Spokes*, no. 48, Autumn 1997.
17. *Evening Standard*, 18 February 1997.
18. *Leicester Spokes*, no. 48, Autumn 1997.
19. John Adams, Mayer Hillman, John Whitelegg, *One False Move*, London: PSI, 1990.
20. Colin Ward, *The Child in the City*, London: Bedford Square, 1990, second edn.
21. *Daily Telegraph*, 22 November 1997.
22. *The Times*, 22 November 1997.
23. *New Times*, 14 September 1996.
24. *Police Stop!*, London: Labyrinth Media, 1994.
25. *Lancashire Evening Post*, 4 March 1996.
26. *Leicester Mercury*, 28 February 1996.

Chapter Nine: The highwaymen business

1. Institute of Advanced Motorists.
2. Jeremy Clarkson, *Hot 100: Cars That Make You Go Phwoar!*, London: Virgin, 1997.
3. *Right to Reply*, Channel 4, 4 October 1997.
4. RoSPA press release, 11 August 1997.
5. *Mirror*, 8 August 1997.
6. *Auto Express*, 28 November 1997.
7. Ashden Trust, *Companies and Cars*, July 1997.
8. Ibid.
9. Ibid.
10. Ibid.
11. Ashden Trust, *Companies and Cars*.
12. Monks Partnership, *Company Car Policy UK 1996*, 1996.

Chapter Ten: Allo, John, got a new motor?

1. *Economist*, 22 June 1996.
2. Perkin, *The Age of the Automobile*, p. 228.
3. *Going Green*, no. 28, Spring 1997.
4. *Mother Jones*, March/April 1997.
5. *Encyclopedia Britannica*, Macropaedia, no. 28, Chicago, Encyclopedia Britannica, 15th edn, 1997.
6. Ibid.
7. Michael Redclift, *From Wasted: Counting the Costs of Global Consumption*, London: Earthscan, 1997.
8. *New Statesman*, 14 November 1997.
9. Jacques Legrand, *Chronicle of the 20th Century*, France, J.L. International Publications, 1988.
10. Marsh and Collett, *Driving Passion*.
11. *Auto Express*, 24 September 1997.

12.   *Auto Express*, 15 October 1997.

13.   *The Times*, 24 November 1997.

14.   *Independent*, 14 August 1996.

15.   *Evening Standard*, 10 February 1998.

16.   *Time*, Our Precious Planet, Special Issue 1997.

17.   *Daily Mail,* 16 December 1997.

18.   *Economist*, 22 June 1996.

19.   *Daily Telegraph*, 19 April 1997.

20.   *Daily Mail,* 16 December 1997.

21.   *Blue Peter*, BBC1, 28 November 1997.

22.   *Time*, New Age of Discovery, 1997.

23.   Whitelegg, *Critical Mass*.

24.   *Time*, Our Precious Planet, Special Issue, 1997.

25.   *BBC Top Gear* magazine, November 1996.

26.   *Mirror*, 11 July 1997.

27.   *Mirror*, 5 July 1997.

28.   *The Times*, 20 December 1997.

29.   *Economist*, 10 May 1997.

30.   *Economist*, 22 June 1996.

31.   *Auto Express*, 24 September 1997.

Chapter Eleven: The estate we're in

1.   *Independent*, 30 December 1997.

2.   *Sunday Times*, 16 November 1997.

3.   Keats, *The Insolent Chariots*.

WINTERDANCE

The Fine Madness of Alaskan Dog-Racing

Gary Paulsen

'Brilliant . . . As much about one man's obsession as about the frozen tundra, the acclaimed adventure writer's crackingly readable book goes a long way towards explaining why people compete in such insane undertakings'   Stephen Amidon, *Esquire*

'Non-stop, breathtaking excitement as sparsely written as the bleak, frozen Arctic landscape it describes . . . Paulsen has given us a wonderful story, full of humour, pathos, adventure, seat-gripping excitement – and a glimpse into the mind of a man in love with his environment and his fellow creatures'

Bruce Sandison, *Glasgow Herald*

'It is hard to find a page in this laconic book without an insight, hard to find a word that could be cut without loss. WINTERDANCE is beautiful and it is very funny and it is about men and dogs and their souls'   *Washington Post*

'In a rapidly shrinking world, there can be few stories of genuinely original adventure still to be written. WINTERDANCE may prove to be one of the last, but also one of the best'

Andrew Shields, *Time Out*

ISBN 0 575 40008 0

*IND*IGO

EASTERN SUN, WINTER MOON

Gary Paulsen

Gary Paulsen's astonishing memoir of a wartime childhood tells of his journey with his mother, who is alternately fiercely protective and selfishly neglectful, from Chicago to the Philippines, where the pair have been summoned by his father, a distant and imperious army officer who Gary has never known. Scenes of extreme horror – such as a bloody encounter with sharks in the Pacific – alternate with tender evocations of the life of a young boy. It ranks with the greatest of twentieth-century childhood memoirs.

'In its raw portrayal of a child thrown into the horrors of war and the adult world, this book reminds one of J. G. Ballard's *Empire of the Sun*'   Tim Winton, *Los Angeles Times*

'Richly evocative, flawlessly observed and profoundly moving . . . Paulsen's lean, spare, conversational style never strays from the voice of the child, yet resonates between the lines with a wisdom and perception beyond his years. EASTERN SUN, WINTER MOON is a quiet masterpiece'   Mick Brown, *Daily Telegraph*

ISBN 0 575 40069 2

*IND*IGO

OVER THE EDGE

A regular guy's odyssey in extreme sports

Michael Bane

'A "regular guy" . . . one day puts together a list of 13 high-risk sports – and then goes off and does 'em . . . Gripping and often hilarious reading. You'll be making your own list in no time'

Pete Muir, *Maxim*

'Enthralling' Maris Ross, *Daily Mail*

'Tackling the list cost him $30,000 and one girlfriend, he says – but it has provided him with the material for a thrilling and unusual book'

Graham Sharpe, *All Sport and Leisure Monthly*

'He is modest, and without his gurus . . . he would never have made it beyond chapter four. "Vigorous risks, wilfully undertaken," he calls his enterprises. To give you some idea: on the Kamikaze downhill race. "What happens if I let go and can't stop?" I ask. "Silly Michael," says Karen. "You go off the mountain, and you die."' *Economist*

ISBN 0 575 40085 4

*IND*IGO

REFLECTIONS OF EDEN

My Life with the Orangutans of Borneo

Biruté M. F. Galdikas

Dian Fossey and her gorillas; Jane Goodall and her chimpanzees; and now, the third of the 'trimates', Biruté Galdikas, who has devoted her adult life to studying and protecting the orangutans of Borneo. This is the enthralling story of a pioneering primatologist, a world leader in conservation – and a remarkable woman.

'Brilliant . . . Galdikas is a born storyteller, disarmingly frank about herself and her subjects . . . But Galdikas's tale is more than storytelling. It is the best possible advertisement for the rainforest. No amount of angry politics and tedious United Nationizing can have half as much practical effect as one really good, gripping account like this'   Matt Ridley, *Sunday Telegraph*

'Now there must be a place for orangutans in the heart of the world'
David Bellamy

'It is a familiar warning. But seldom has it been spelt out with such impassioned clarity'   Brian Jackman, *The Times*

'You will be transported to another world. And you won't forget'
Jane Goodall

ISBN 0 575 40002 1

*IN*D*I*GO

PLAGUE'S PROGRESS
A Social History of Man and Disease

Arno Karlen

Winner of the 1996 Rhône-Poulenc Prize for Science Books

'Chock-full of the most devastating accounts of plagues and graphic descriptions of the diseases which cause them . . . Blood-curdling'
Harriet Stewart, *Guardian*

'Excellent. It is the most frightening (and sobering) book I have seen since *How We Die*, and leaves one wondering about the nature of "progress", and how – as a species – we ever managed to survive. I think the combination of meticulous research and easy, natural writing makes the drama of this horrid reality even more intense'
Oliver Sacks

'While avoiding hysteria, Karlen's clear, complete survey affirms the total involvement of our fate as humans with the wider health of the planet. It's a lesson our grasping, reckless and short-sighted species must learn fast'
Roy Porter, *Observer*

'Arno Karlen efficiently and convincingly converts the apocalyptic good of infectious disease into strong historical currency . . . His case is difficult to refute'
Richard Horton, *New Scientist*

ISBN 0 575 40012 9

*I*ND*I*GO

THE HIDDEN WIRING
Unearthing the British Constitution

Peter Hennessy

Peter Hennesy is a demystifier who for twenty years has been searching for the concealed codes of state power, and in THE HIDDEN WIRING he unravels the mysteries of the British constitution to expose the true nature of the relationships between the five institutions at the core of public life: Monarchy, Premiership, Cabinet, Whitehall and Parliament. With the conduct of public affairs under scrutiny as never before, Peter Hennessy's characteristic wit, zest and incisiveness have never been deployed to better effect.

'Hennessy's discussion of his separate themes is . . . brimming with scholarship and erudition. He writes, as he speaks on both radio and television, with pace and verve' Anthony Howard, *Spectator*

'Characteristically timely, lively and provocative'
David Cannadine, *Observer*

'The vibrant tones of the author's infectious enthusiasm ring from every page' Julia Langdon, *Glasgow Herald*

'The irreplaceable analyst of the inner core of the British system of government' Andrew Marr, I*ndependent*

ISBN 0 575 40058 7

*IN*D*I*GO

Out of the blue...
*I*NDIGO
the best in modern writing